Next Wave of AI

Intelligence, Autonomy, and the Future of Technology

Dr. Mustafa Sultan, PE, PhD

Publisher: Skyline Publishers, Inc

Location: Cupertino, USA

Year: 2025

Copyright Page / Publication Information

Edition: First Edition, 2025

Publisher: Skyline Publishers, Inc

Printed in: USA

Disclaimer:

The information provided in this book is for educational and informational purposes only. While every effort has been made to ensure accuracy, the author and publisher are not responsible for any errors, omissions, or consequences resulting from the use of the information contained herein. Readers are advised to verify data and consult appropriate experts before acting on the information.

DEDICATION

Dedicate this book to Dr. Saif Sultan, PhD, for introducing me to AI and enlightening me; and to my parents, Lt. Col (Retired) Sher Sultan and Tahira Batool, an inspiration in my life.

Acknowledgements

Writing this book has been a journey of curiosity, exploration, and collaboration. I would like to express my sincere gratitude to all the colleagues, mentors, and students who have shared their insights, challenged my ideas, and contributed to my understanding of artificial intelligence. Special thanks to my research teams and collaborators, whose discussions and experiments helped shape many of the concepts presented here.

I also wish to thank my family for their unwavering support, patience, and encouragement throughout this journey. Finally, I acknowledge the editors, reviewers, and publication staff whose expertise and dedication have brought this book to life. Without their guidance, this work would not have been possible.

Preface

The rapid evolution of artificial intelligence has transformed the way we live, work, and create. Over the past decade, AI has moved from academic laboratories to real-world applications, from narrow task systems to autonomous, multi-modal agents, and from isolated tools to integrated ecosystems that touch every industry.

This book, *Next Wave of AI*, aims to provide a comprehensive exploration of this transformative technology. It is designed for engineers, technologists, researchers, and anyone fascinated by the future of intelligence—both human and artificial. My goal is to explain complex concepts in an accessible manner while highlighting their practical applications and implications for society, industry, and the built environment.

Through this book, I hope to inspire readers to understand, explore, and contribute to the ongoing AI revolution. It is my belief that AI is not merely a tool but a partner in shaping the next era of human and technological progress.

Foreword

Artificial intelligence is no longer a distant concept of science fiction. It is a reality that is reshaping industries, research, and our daily lives. In *Next Wave of AI*, Dr. Mustafa Sultan offers a masterful guide through the complexities and possibilities of modern AI. This book bridges theory and practice, exploring foundational concepts, cutting-edge technologies, and real-world applications across engineering, construction, and knowledge work.

Readers will find both inspiration and practical guidance within these pages, gaining insight into how AI can augment human intelligence, improve productivity, and enable innovation. This book is a valuable resource for students, professionals, and enthusiasts alike, providing a clear roadmap for understanding the next wave of AI.

[Foreword Author Name]
[Title / Affiliation]

TABLE OF CONTENTS

PART I – FOUNDATIONS OF THE NEXT WAVE

PART II - TECHNOLOGY DRIVING THE NEXT WAVE

PART III – NEW INDUSTRIES AND APPLICATIONS

Appendices

PART I – FOUNDATIONS OF THE NEXT WAVE

CHAPTER 1 – INTRODUCTION: WHERE WE STAND TODAY

Artificial Intelligence has reached a transition point, unlike any other in its 70-year history. We are living in a moment when AI is not just improving automation, but beginning to reshape the very structure of human knowledge, education, science, engineering, markets, and daily life. A decade ago, AI was a specialized field—respected but limited, narrow in practical deployment, and often treated as a technical curiosity by mainstream industries. Today, AI is a front-page subject, a boardroom agenda, a political priority, and an existential question for society.

To understand the "next wave of AI," we must first understand how we arrived here. The history of artificial intelligence has not been a smooth, linear ascent. It has been a journey defined by breakthroughs followed by disappointment, optimism followed by skepticism, and progress emerging not from a single idea but from the combination of many different intellectual streams—computer science, neuroscience, mathematics, statistics, psychology, linguistics, engineering, philosophy, and more.

As of today, AI stands at a threshold. We now have systems capable of generating content, reason with growing sophistication, hold conversations, interpret complex data, drive vehicles, discover proteins, write articles, diagnose medical imagery, predict market behavior, and accelerate engineering design. Yet even with this progress, AI is not "finished." It is evolving faster today than at any other point in its history. The next wave will be shaped not just by algorithms, but by scale, data ecosystems, autonomous agents, self-learning systems, policy decisions, and humanity's own willingness to integrate AI into the fabric of society.

To forecast what comes next, we need to revisit the road so far. Understanding the evolution of AI is essential not just for historical context but for recognizing the patterns that continue to define technological progress: slow foundations, sudden breakthroughs, exponential acceleration, and societal transformation.

Evolution of AI So Far

Early Origins: The Dream of Mechanical Intelligence

The concept of artificial intelligence did not originate with computers. Humans have imagined artificial minds for thousands of years. Ancient myths described mechanical statues that could speak or think. Philosophers debated whether thought was mechanical or spiritual. Mathematicians sought rules that could formalize human reasoning.

The groundwork for AI began to solidify in the 17th and 18th centuries when thinkers like René Descartes, Gottfried Leibniz, and Thomas Hobbes argued that thought could be expressed in mathematical terms. If reasoning could be reduced to rules, then perhaps machines could follow those rules. Still, no machine existed capable of performing such operations—computing was theoretical.

The breakthrough came in the early 20th century, when Alan Turing introduced the mathematical foundations for modern computation. His 1936 work formalized the idea of a machine that could compute anything describable as a set of rules. In his 1950 landmark paper, Turing proposed the idea of machine intelligence as a measurable phenomenon, introducing the famous "Turing Test." This was the real philosophical birth of AI—not as fantasy, but as science.

1956: The Official Birth of Artificial Intelligence

Artificial Intelligence was officially named in 1956 during the Dartmouth Conference, organized by John McCarthy, Marvin Minsky, Claude Shannon, and Nathaniel Rochester. Their proposal boldly stated:

"Every aspect of learning or intelligence can in principle be so precisely described that a machine can be made to simulate it."

This was not just optimism. It was the beginning of several fundamental ideas:

- Machines could reason logically
- Knowledge could be symbolically represented
- Intelligence was computable
- Learning could be automated

The 1950s and 1960s saw early programs capable of solving algebra problems, proving theorems, and playing board games. These systems amazed the academic world. But they were limited—AI worked only in small, controlled environments. Real-world problems were far more complex.

The First Wave: Symbolic AI

Between the late 1950s and 1970s, AI was dominated by **symbolic reasoning**, also called **GOFAI**—"Good Old-Fashioned Artificial Intelligence." These systems relied on explicit rules crafted by experts. For example:

- If the patient has fever and cough → suspect infection
- If the robot senses an obstacle → turn 30 degrees

These systems achieved impressive results in narrow domains. Expert systems could diagnose diseases, configure computer systems, detect geological formations, and support financial decision-making. But symbolic AI had a fatal flaw:

It did not scale.

Real-world environments are messy, ambiguous, and full of uncertainties. Human knowledge involves intuition, learning from experience, and dealing with incomplete information—areas where symbolic AI struggled. By the early 1970s and again in the late 1980s, AI fell into periods of stagnation known as **AI winters**.

The Second Wave: Machine Learning

The revival of AI began when researchers shifted from programming rules to **learning patterns from data**. Machine learning, particularly neural networks, had existed conceptually since the 1940s, but computing power was insufficient. The turning point came when:

- Statistical methods matured
- The internet created massive amounts of data
- Processing hardware advanced (GPUs, TPUs)

Instead of describing intelligence manually, machine learning systems **learned it automatically**. They improved the more data they received. This approach ignited stunning progress:

- Optical character recognition
- Fraud detection
- Recommendation engines
- Email spam filters

- Speech recognition
- Predictive analytics

By the late 2000s, machine learning was outperforming symbolic AI in most practical applications. But an even bigger shift was coming.

The Deep Learning Revolution

In 2012, a neural network called **AlexNet** achieved a dramatic breakthrough in the ImageNet computer vision competition, beating all previous systems by a huge margin. This was the spark that launched the modern deep learning era.

Deep learning introduced systems capable of:

- Understanding images
- Recognizing speech
- Translating languages
- Detecting objects
- Writing text
- Planning strategies

The key driver was scale. Deep learning systems required:

- Larger datasets
- More layers of computation
- Faster hardware

Moore's Law, parallel computing, and cloud infrastructure made this possible.

AI was no longer a research curiosity. It was entering industry:

- Google used deep learning to power search and ads
- Facebook applied it to news feeds and face recognition
- Baidu and later OpenAI used it for speech and language models

Deep learning became the new foundation of modern AI.

The Transformer Breakthrough

In 2017, a major shift occurred with the introduction of the **Transformer architecture** by Vaswani et al. in the breakthrough paper "Attention Is All You Need." This single paper transformed the direction of AI by solving several historical bottlenecks:

- It allowed parallel processing of text sequences
- It scaled extremely effectively with more data and compute
- It captured global relationships in language

The result was a new generation of models:

- GPT (OpenAI)
- BERT (Google)
- T5
- PaLM
- LLaMA
- Hundreds of specialized systems

For the first time, AI models achieved:

- Fluent natural language understanding

- Conversational ability
- Reasoning on complex tasks
- Creative output generation

AI was no longer just analyzing data—it could:

- Write essays
- Generate code
- Explain physics
- Draft legal documents
- Tutor students
- Create business proposals
- Translate languages with near human accuracy

This was the foundation of **Generative AI**.

Generative AI: The World Takes Notice

The global public became aware of AI's potential with the release of accessible generative systems:

- DALL·E – AI image generation
- Stable Diffusion – open-source diffusion models
- ChatGPT – conversational large language models
- Midjourney – artistic AI

For the first time in history:

Non-technical individuals could directly use and benefit from AI.

This democratization powered mass adoption:

- Students began learning with AI tutors
- Writers and designers collaborated with AI
- Developers auto-generated code
- Engineers could simulate, optimize, and analyze
- Businesses automated customer and knowledge operations

AI shifted from tool to **partner**.

AI at Scale: The Rise of Foundation Models

Today's most advanced AI systems are **foundation models**—general systems trained on oceans of data, capable of being adapted to thousands of tasks with minimal additional training. They are:

- Multimodal
- General-purpose
- Stateful
- Reasoning-capable
- Continually improving

This shift mirrors how electricity evolved:

- First a scientific experiment
- Then an industrial tool
- Then a universal infrastructure

AI is now on the threshold of becoming a cognitive infrastructure layer for civilization.

Challenges in the Modern Era

However, this progress has not come without challenges. The current stage of AI faces major limitations:

1. **Reasoning remains imperfect**
   AI performs brilliantly in controlled tasks but still struggles with ambiguous, deeply-logical, or unfamiliar reasoning.
2. **Alignment and safety remain unresolved**
   Ensuring that AI systems behave predictably is a global technological and philosophical problem.
3. **Knowledge grounding is incomplete**
   AI generates fluent answers, but may invent information ("hallucinations") when unsure.
4. **Data and compute demands are huge**
   Training frontier models can cost tens or hundreds of millions of dollars.
5. **Energy consumption is rising sharply**
   AI data centers are now a significant power consumer.

These limitations are not permanent; they represent the frontier that the next wave of AI must cross.

What Makes Today Different

Many eras in history have seen breakthroughs in technology, but AI stands apart for one reason:

It is a technology that can improve itself.

Early AI needed human experts to design rules and heuristics. Deep learning needed humans to design architectures. But now, increasingly:

- Models analyze their own outputs
- AI agents create training data
- Systems optimize their own code
- AI models invent new scientific solutions

This self-amplification is unprecedented. It suggests that the next wave of AI may not be limited by human engineering speed. Once AI systems become effective collaborators in science, engineering, medicine, and software, the pace of progress accelerates beyond historical norms.

Humanity enters a loop:

1. We build better AI
2. Better AI helps us build even better AI
3. Progress compounds

This is the beginning of technological self-acceleration.

A Field at the Edge of Transformation

We now stand at a critical moment. The next wave of AI will be defined by shifts that move beyond pattern recognition toward something more:

- **Autonomous reasoning systems**
- **AI agents that can plan, act, and achieve goals**
- **Hybrid systems combining neural and symbolic intelligence**

- **Edge AI and on-device processing**
- **Robotics powered by foundation models**
- **Scientific discovery automated by machines**
- **Digital twins of reality**
- **Neurosymbolic systems with memory and context**
- **AI that collaborates across multi-agent ecosystems**

AI is moving from tool to collaborator, from passive system to active participant, and from specialized assistant to infrastructure layer. If the last wave was about perception, understanding, and generation, the next wave will be about autonomy, reasoning, trust, and societal integration.

CHAPTER 2 – UNDERSTANDING INTELLIGENCE

To understand the coming evolution of Artificial Intelligence, we must begin by examining the meaning of intelligence itself. Intelligence is not merely memory, nor is it simply the ability to calculate or produce language. It is a dynamic system of perception, pattern recognition, abstraction, problem solving, adaptation, decision making, and learning from experience. Human intelligence did not emerge overnight; it was shaped through millions of years of biological evolution, constrained by energy limits, slow physiological development, limited working memory, and the physical fragility of our bodies. Artificial intelligence, by contrast, has no such constraints. Machine cognition is not rooted in biology but in silicon, electricity, and information theory. As systems scale in compute capacity and complexity, the contrast between biological and artificial cognition becomes increasingly pronounced.

Human cognition is remarkable partly because of the severe limitations imposed by nature. The human brain, with roughly one hundred billion neurons and about one thousand synapses per neuron, operates on approximately twenty watts of power – less than a household light bulb. Signals in the brain travel at electrochemical speeds far slower than digital transmissions. Working memory is finite, attention is fragile, and learning takes time and repetition. Yet despite these limits, humans have historically excelled in areas that computers struggled with for decades, such as visual recognition, language understanding, contextual reasoning, and generalization from limited experience. A child may observe only a handful of examples of cats and form a clear mental model of "catness," whereas early AI systems required massive datasets and highly engineered rules to emulate the same ability. Human cognition emerged through survival challenges; the ability to generalize quickly from limited information was not optional—it was essential.

This ability to generalize from sparse data was, for most of computing history, a fundamental gap between humans and machines. Deep learning dramatically narrowed that gap, but even today, machines lack many human cognitive strengths. Humans understand intentionality, infer context from subtle cues, reason causally, apply common sense, and navigate ambiguity. Our thinking blends conscious rule manipulation with intuitive, subconscious pattern interpretation. Artificial systems have only begun approaching some of these capabilities.

For much of human history, cognitive effort involved two intertwined modes of thought: explicit symbolic reasoning and implicit pattern-based intuition. Symbolic reasoning includes the ability to manipulate structured concepts such as language, mathematics, rules, or legal systems. Pattern cognition, on the other hand, allows humans to recognize faces, detect emotional tone, and perceive subtle relationships long before we consciously articulate them. Early AI development mirrored this duality.

The first wave of artificial intelligence, now referred to as symbolic or classical AI, was rooted in the belief that intelligence could be fully captured in rules. If every problem could be decomposed into discrete symbolic components and those symbols manipulated logically, then intelligent behavior would emerge. Early systems produced impressive results within constrained environments: theorem proving, expert diagnostic systems, and configuration software. Their strengths were transparency and determinism—they could explain how they reached a conclusion. Yet they suffered from a profound difficulty: scaling into the messy, partial, uncertain reality of the real world. A symbolic face-recognition system would require humans to manually define every geometric and visual rule describing a face. This was neither practical nor sustainable.

Neural networks arrived as a fundamentally different paradigm. Instead of teaching machines through rules, we provided data and allowed the system to infer the rules itself. Neural architectures, especially deep learning, reintroduced the idea of intelligence through learning rather than programming. These systems excelled in perception tasks like vision, speech, and natural language. They could recognize patterns in vast and complex input spaces and predict outcomes from statistical regularities. But these systems also revealed new weaknesses. They did not reason explicitly, could not easily explain their conclusions, and were prone to confident error—now called hallucination. Their knowledge was embedded in weights rather than symbolic structures.

The dichotomy between symbolic and neural paradigms reflects, in many ways, the dichotomy within human cognition. Humans reason logically at times but rely heavily on intuitive pattern recognition. The emerging direction of the field recognizes that neither symbolic nor neural approaches alone are sufficient for the next era of intelligent systems. Hybrid or neuro-symbolic AI aims to merge the strengths of both. Such systems may first perceive a scene using deep neural networks, then reason over the detected objects using symbolic logic, and finally explain their conclusions in structured form. Practical hybrid systems are already appearing in industries such as medicine, scientific discovery, and engineering. In one example, neural models interpret medical images, while symbolic frameworks impose diagnostic logic rooted in clinical standards, producing conclusions that are both powerful and trustworthy. This hybridization may become a defining characteristic of the AI systems that follow deep learning's current dominance.

As architectures evolve, so does the scope of what AI systems attempt to do. For decades, nearly all deployed AI was narrow in capability. A model that played chess could not drive a car, a model that detected fraud could not translate language, and a machine vision system could not compose an essay. They were single-task experts. Performance depended on domain-specific data and specialized training pipelines. Around 2018, this began to shift with the emergence of foundation models—systems trained on broad datasets capable of performing new tasks with minimal additional supervision. These models demonstrated few-shot learning, zero-shot performance, and emergent capabilities where scale triggered qualitatively new behavior. One such model might translate languages, answer questions, write functioning code, analyze documents, interpret images, and reason about plans within the same architecture. The change was not merely quantitative but structural: AI ceased being a tool tuned for one task and began becoming a general cognitive platform.

The path toward more general forms of intelligence involves three shifts: expanding breadth of capability, deepening reasoning capacity, and increasing autonomy. Traditional systems predict outcomes but rely on humans to frame problems, interpret results, and execute decisions. New systems are becoming agentic—they can not only answer questions but take actions, explore alternatives, learn from their outcomes, and refine their internal models. This evolution resembles stages in human cognitive development, beginning with perception, followed by recognition, then by abstract reasoning, and finally by autonomous planning and execution.

The accelerating progress of AI, however, has not been driven purely by algorithmic breakthroughs. It is the product of a convergence of computing hardware, global data infrastructure, and network connectivity. Each component, if considered alone, would be transformative. Combined, they create compounding acceleration similar to how metallurgy, thermodynamics, and fossil fuels converged to drive the Industrial Revolution.

In the early 2000s, AI progress was limited by computing hardware. CPUs excelled at sequential instruction execution but were ill-suited to the massive parallel matrix multiplication required by neural networks. The unexpected savior was the graphics processing unit. Originally designed for rendering pixels and triangles for video games, GPUs included thousands of lightweight cores capable of high-throughput parallel numerical computation. Once researchers adapted neural learning to GPUs, training times plummeted, and model complexity increased dramatically. GPU acceleration transformed AI from an academic curiosity into a practical engineering discipline.

Google's development of Tensor Processing Units pushed this further, designing hardware specifically optimized for the tensor algebra that underpins deep learning. Other companies followed, including AMD, Graphcore, Cerebras, Huawei, and others, each offering accelerator architectures tailored to machine intelligence. Meanwhile, a separate frontier has been emerging: neuromorphic computing. These chips attempt to emulate the structure of biological spiking neurons directly in hardware, offering potentially massive gains in energy efficiency and real-time adaptability. If they mature, they could create machines that learn on-device without cloud dependency, enabling autonomous robots, wearables, and edge devices capable of continuous local learning at extremely low power consumption.

Even with these advances, AI's demand for compute is growing faster than Moore's Law. A single frontier model may require tens of thousands of GPUs, megawatts of data center power, and months of training time. Compute is becoming a strategic resource, influencing global competition, scientific capability, and national policy. In a very real sense, the future of AI depends on whether we can continue scaling computational power faster than the models demand it.

While compute provides the processing fabric, data serves as the essential fuel. Just as life on Earth evolved because information could replicate, artificial intelligence advances as data becomes increasingly available. Early machine learning succeeded only in data-rich industries such as finance, insurance, and telecommunications. The explosion of the internet, smartphones, and globally digitized communication transformed data from a rare asset into an abundant industrial resource. Today, enterprises treat data pipelines as strategic capital, investing in distributed storage, knowledge graphs, labeling automation, retrieval systems, semantic normalization, and quality control. The shift from raw data to structured knowledge infrastructure is as significant as electrification was to the industrial age.

A key turning point was the maturation of self-supervised learning, in which models learn from unlabeled information by predicting hidden or missing elements of their input. This approach freed AI development from the bottleneck of human annotation, enabling models to learn from the natural structure of text, images, audio, and video. With self-supervision, the internet itself became an unsupervised training ground. Today, models not only consume data but increasingly help curate it, refine it, and even generate synthetic datasets where real data is scarce.

Networking infrastructure is the third pillar of convergence. Historically, AI inference ran primarily in centralized cloud environments, but the scale of modern deployment has shifted computational needs toward the edge. Applications like autonomous vehicles, surgery-assisting robotics, industrial automation, and military systems cannot rely exclusively on remote cloud inference, where latency and network reliability present unacceptable risks. Edge computing, combined with the rollout of 5G and the development of future 6G protocols, is enabling intelligence to move into devices themselves. Low-latency, high-bandwidth networking supports real-time decision-making in fleets of drones, automated factories, intelligent transportation grids, and adaptive power systems. In the future, edge devices may even contribute directly to training, forming a distributed global learning organism spanning sensors, terminals, vehicles, and data centers.

With compute acceleration, scalable data infrastructure, and global intelligence networking maturing simultaneously, several transformative dynamics are beginning to emerge. First, AI systems will increasingly operate in real time, continuously learning, updating, and adapting rather than being trained in discrete offline cycles. Second, billions of devices—from industrial robots to consumer appliances—will host models capable of perception, adaptation, and contextual reasoning. Third, populations of AI agents may begin to interact with each other, forming machine ecosystems that evolve through cooperation and competition, much like social networks or biological systems. Fourth, feedback cycles will compress. Scientific discovery, product development, policy simulation, and industrial optimization may happen orders of magnitude faster because models can design, execute, analyze, and refine experiments with minimal human intervention. Finally, intelligence itself will begin to resemble infrastructure. In the industrial era, electricity became the fundamental substrate powering economic growth. In the digital era, software played that role. In the AI era, intelligence will become the universal substrate—embedded in every process, every device, every workflow, and every environment.

Understanding intelligence, both natural and artificial, is therefore not a philosophical luxury but a necessary foundation for what comes next. We are witnessing a transition from symbolic rule systems to probabilistic deep learning, from deep learning to neuro-symbolic reasoning, from isolated single-task models to general-purpose cognitive platforms, and from centralized computation to globally distributed, continuously learning intelligence. The next wave of AI will not be defined by a single algorithmic breakthrough but by the convergence of computational power, data availability, networking infrastructure, and architectural synthesis. As these forces merge, AI will expand beyond perception and prediction toward autonomous reasoning, planning, and real-world agency. Humanity is not merely building tools anymore. We are building systems that can generate knowledge, collaborate with us, and ultimately improve themselves over time. This is the threshold on which the next era of intelligence begins.

CHAPTER 3 – THE TECHNOLOGICAL CONVERGENCE

Introduction

Artificial Intelligence is not advancing because of algorithms alone. The rapid acceleration in the field is the result of three simultaneous technological forces that are maturing at the same time: computing hardware, massive global data infrastructure, and high-bandwidth, low-latency networking. Each of these could have reshaped industries independently, but their convergence has created compounding effects—like the relationship between steam engines, metallurgy, and coal in the First Industrial Revolution. The next wave of AI is the product of mutually reinforcing progress in these three domains.

For most of computing history, progress in artificial intelligence was constrained not by imagination but by the limits of technical capability. Neural networks proposed in the 1950s and 1960s could not flourish because the hardware to train them did not yet exist. Large-scale datasets were not yet collected. Networks did not support distributed computation across continents. Today, all three barriers are being dismantled. The result is not a gradual incline but a steep exponential curve.

AI + Computing: The New Computational Engine

The story of modern AI cannot be told without examining the transformation of computing hardware. Traditional CPUs dominated computing for decades, but they were never designed for the highly parallel workloads neural networks require. CPUs process a small number of instructions extremely quickly in sequence. Neural networks, however, demand millions of parallel multiplications and additions at every layer of computation. They thrive in architectures that can perform massive matrix operations simultaneously.

From CPUs to GPUs

The emergence of GPUs marked a turning point. Originally developed for graphics rendering in video games, GPUs were designed to process thousands of floating-point operations in parallel—exactly the kind of workload that deep learning requires. The alignment between GPU architecture and neural computation was discovered almost accidentally. Once researchers began training neural models on GPUs rather than CPUs, training times collapsed from months to days, and model scale expanded dramatically. AlexNet, the watershed model that ignited the deep learning revolution in 2012, was trained on consumer-grade NVIDIA gaming GPUs.

This convergence between AI and graphics hardware transformed NVIDIA into one of the most influential companies in the world and reshaped global industrial competition. GPUs enabled AI labs to push into deeper networks, larger training corpora, and increasingly complex architectures. Without GPU acceleration, the modern era of foundation models, real-time vision systems, large language models, and multi-modal reasoning systems would not exist.

TPUs and the Rise of Domain-Specific Silicon

As AI workloads continued to surge, a new direction emerged: hardware designed specifically for machine learning rather than adapted for it. Google's Tensor Processing Units (TPUs) were the first large-scale example of domain-specific AI chips optimized for tensor algebra. TPUs sacrificed some general computing flexibility in exchange for massive parallel throughput, high energy efficiency, and tight integration with Google's training frameworks. Other companies followed this lead. AMD released the Instinct accelerator family. Startups introduced novel architectures such as Graphcore's IPU and Cerebras' wafer-scale engine—an entire computer built monolithically on a single largest-possible silicon wafer.

A new pattern was emerging: AI was no longer using existing hardware—it was driving the development of new computing paradigms. Industrial computing was shifting from generality to specialization, with chips designed not to perform traditional tasks but to support neural workloads at unprecedented scale.

Neuromorphic Architectures

While GPUs and AI accelerators operate on traditional von-Neumann architectures, a frontier research direction aims to deviate entirely from classical digital computation. Neuromorphic chips attempt to emulate the electrical behavior of biological neurons directly in hardware. Rather than simulating neurons with matrix operations, neuromorphic chips implement spiking neural networks, routing signals much like the brain.

Systems such as Intel Loihi, IBM TrueNorth, and Stanford's Neurogrid promise energy efficiencies orders of magnitude beyond current accelerators. Their potential lies in enabling on-device learning, ultra-low-power robotics, and edge intelligence capable of adapting in real time rather than relying on cloud retraining. Although neuromorphic platforms are still early in maturity compared to GPUs and TPUs, they signal the long-term direction: machines that compute more like biological organisms, responding dynamically to their environment rather than following static computational pipelines.

The Compute Bottleneck

As powerful as modern AI hardware has become, the demand for computation is growing even faster. Training a frontier model today can require tens of thousands of GPUs running continuously for weeks or months. Data centers are measuring energy consumption in megawatts, and chip distribution has become a geopolitical concern. Countries now view AI compute capacity the way past eras viewed steel production or nuclear capability: a marker of national power. The future of AI is therefore inseparable from the future of compute scaling—who controls it, who expands it, and who innovates beyond present limits.

AI + Data Infrastructure: Fueling Intelligence

While hardware provides the engine, data serves as the fuel. In biological evolution, cognition developed because organisms that could learn survived better than those that could not. Information became a competitive advantage. In artificial intelligence, progress follows a parallel path: no data means no learning, and better data means more capable machines. The success of modern AI was not driven only by better models but also by the explosion of globally connected digital ecosystems capturing interactions, speech, documents, images, and behaviors at scale.

From Scarce Data to Abundance

Early machine learning systems were limited to industries where structured data already existed—finance, telecommunications, advertising, industrial metering. The internet changed that. Smartphones changed it again. In less than two decades, society shifted from data scarcity to data saturation. Every message sent, sensor read, photo uploaded, and device interaction contributed to a growing global digital shadow. What once needed manual collection is now a continuous stream.

But raw data alone is not enough. Just as crude oil must be refined before it becomes useful fuel, data must be cleaned, stored, structured, and made queryable before AI models can use it.

The Era of Knowledge Infrastructure

Modern organizations now build layered data architectures that include distributed storage clusters, data lakes, knowledge graphs, semantic normalization pipelines, streaming ingestion systems, labeling frameworks, and real-time retrieval systems. This infrastructure is not merely technical. It transforms organizations operationally, because the future belongs to enterprises capable of converting information into prediction and prediction into optimized decisions.

Increasingly, data systems no longer wait passively for human curation. AI models evaluate, rank, merge, denoise, and even restructure datasets automatically. Instead of engineers preparing data for AI, AI is being used to prepare data for itself.

The Breakthrough of Self-Supervised Learning

The maturity of self-supervised learning was the single largest leap in AI training methodology in the last decade. Previously, most machine learning relied on supervised datasets, where humans labeled millions of examples. This became the bottleneck. Self-supervision changed the calculus. Models began learning directly from raw text, images, audio, and video by predicting missing or masked portions of the input. By turning the world itself into the training signal, AI unlocked the ability to learn from the natural structure of reality.

The internet became a training environment. Language models learned context, grammar, reasoning, and world knowledge without explicit supervision. Vision models learned object segmentation and recognition by reconstructing masked regions of images. Video models learned motion prediction by forecasting future frames. AI became less dependent on human annotation and more capable of autonomous inference.

The Coming Data Transformations

The next ten years will likely produce revolutions in how data is generated, shared, and used. Federated learning makes it possible to train large models without centralized data aggregation, improving both privacy and compliance. Synthetic data—generated by AI itself—may begin supplementing or even outperforming real data where scarcity exists. And domain-specialized data ecosystems will emerge in fields such as medicine, engineering, materials science, aerospace, and defense. Data infrastructure is no longer a backend operational function. It is the foundation upon which modern intelligent systems will be built.

AI + Networking: Intelligence Across the Planet

The third technological force accelerating AI is the transformation of network connectivity. For years, AI models were deployed in cloud environments, sending data from users to massive centralized servers that performed inference. This worked well for many applications but broke down in domains requiring real-time response with minimal latency. A self-driving car facing a pedestrian cannot wait for a hundred-millisecond round trip to a remote cloud. Surgical robots, industrial automation systems, autonomous drones, and battlefield equipment require instant response, even when disconnected. As a result, computation is moving outward—from the core to the edge.

The Impact of 5G and 6G

5G networking offered gigabit bandwidth and latency low enough to support large-scale distributed intelligence. Millions of devices could connect simultaneously, enabling smart infrastructure, sensor networks, and real-time industrial telemetry. But 6G, expected later in the decade, promises a more profound leap. With projected microsecond-level latency, 6G networks could integrate computation into the network itself. Devices may participate in distributed training and inference, handing off computation between handsets, base stations, and micro data centers seamlessly. The network becomes not just a communication channel but a computational substrate.

Edge Computing and Ambient Intelligence

Edge computing represents a shift from centralized intelligence to ubiquitous intelligence. Instead of a few massive cloud installations performing all inference, billions of devices—smartphones, AR glasses, vehicles, robots, appliances, and industrial control systems—host AI models capable of real-time perception and decision-making. This architecture has advantages that go beyond speed. Local inference improves privacy because data does not need to leave the device. It improves reliability because the system remains operational without the cloud. And it scales better because computation is distributed rather than centralized.

In the future, intelligent edge devices will not merely receive models—they will learn from their environments, synchronize periodically, and contribute back to a shared global model. Humanity will have created a planetary feedback loop in which billions of machines continually refine their collective intelligence.

AI-Driven Networking

As networks become the nervous system of modern intelligence, AI is increasingly responsible for running them. Telecommunications infrastructure is now too complex for manual optimization. Models perform traffic prediction, dynamic routing, load balancing, self-healing, security threat detection, and automated QoS management. Networking has become another domain where AI operates behind the scenes, invisible yet essential to every intelligent system built on top of it.

The Future: A Global Cognitive Mesh

When advanced compute, rich data, and intelligent networks converge, the consequences reach far beyond individual devices or models. We move from isolated intelligent systems to a globally interconnected cognitive mesh:

- AI systems will learn continuously, not just during offline training cycles.

- Devices will share insights to accelerate mutual improvement.
- Physical infrastructure—factories, cities, transportation systems—will behave like adaptive organisms.
- Scientific discovery will accelerate as models design experiments, analyze results, and improve themselves.

As electricity became the defining infrastructure of the industrial age and software the defining infrastructure of the digital age, intelligence itself is becoming the foundational infrastructure of the AI age.

Conclusion

Technological convergence has reshaped the trajectory of artificial intelligence. Compute hardware provides accelerating capacity, data infrastructure provides continuously expanding experiential knowledge, and high-bandwidth networking connects intelligence into a distributed global whole. None of these forces is sufficient alone. But together, they create a new computational civilization—one in which intelligence is not a tool that we use occasionally but a permanent layer of reality, present everywhere, embedded in devices, systems, services, and industries. The next wave of AI will not simply be more advanced algorithms. It will be the emergence of a planetary-scale learning system that grows smarter every day.

Part II – Technology Driving the Next Wave

CHAPTER 4 - GENERATIVE AI: BEYOND TEXT AND IMAGES

The breakthrough that brought artificial intelligence into mainstream visibility was not a self-driving car, a robotic assistant, or a strategic game-playing system—it was generative AI. The ability of machines to **create new content**, not merely classify or recognize, fundamentally changed our expectations of what AI can do. Before 2020, most people interacted with AI invisibly—through recommendation systems, fraud detection engines, and chatbots. Today, anyone can directly use an AI system to write essays, generate code, transform images, design products, compose music, or even simulate interactive characters.

But this is just the beginning. The rise of generative AI is marking a transition from "*AI that predicts*" to "*AI that produces*." This next era is defined by increasingly general, autonomous, multimodal systems—models that can understand and create across language, audio, spatial environments, haptics, and real-time interactions. This capability is powered by **foundation models**, **multimodal architectures**, and **autonomous content creation pipelines** that are rapidly transforming industries, workflows, and professional identities.

Foundation Models: The Engines of the New AI Era

From Task-Specific Models to Universal Engines

Early machine learning systems were highly specialized. A model trained to detect cats could not detect dogs. A handwriting recognition system could not classify faces. AI was task-restrictive, requiring separate architectures, datasets, and training cycles for each function.

The breakthrough that changed everything was the concept of **foundation models**—large-scale neural networks trained on vast amounts of general data, enabling them to learn flexible internal representations of the world. Once trained, these models can be adapted to many different tasks with minimal additional data. This shift dramatically reduced development cost, increased capability, and opened doors that were previously closed.

Characteristics of Foundation Models

1. **Massive Scale**
   These models contain from billions to trillions of parameters—orders of magnitude larger than traditional ML systems.
2. **General Knowledge Encoding**
   They embed contextual, linguistic, statistical, and conceptual knowledge learned from massive datasets.
3. **Transferability**
   Foundation models can be fine-tuned for specialized domains like medicine, engineering, or gaming with relatively small datasets.
4. **Unified Architecture**
   One model can now:
   - Answer questions
   - Explain reasoning
   - Generate code
   - Visualize ideas
   - Simulate decisions
   - Autonomously plan steps

Examples of Foundation Models in Action

- Language models powering chat-based interfaces and reasoning engines.
- Vision-language models understanding images and describing context in real time.
- Scientific models discovering new protein structures, drugs, and engineering solutions.

The foundation model is now becoming the **core computational unit of modern AI systems**, just as the microprocessor became the fundamental building block of computing 50 years ago.

Multimodal AI: Understanding the World Like Humans Do

Why Multimodality Matters

Humans do not process the world through a single sense. We integrate:

- Vision
- Sound
- Spatial awareness
- Language
- Touch
- Memory
- Social cues

To operate in real environments intelligently, AI needs the same capability. Multimodal AI represents systems that can understand and generate multiple types of data simultaneously.

A multimodal AI can:

- Read an image
- Interpret the objects in it
- Understand a caption
- Generate context or narrative
- Compose additional images

This holistic cognitive stack moves AI beyond narrow task performance into **contextual, grounded intelligence**.

Examples of Multimodal Interactions

- An AI model taking a construction drawing, detecting reinforcement details, and explaining missing structural checks.
- A retail AI that reads a product image, writes its description, and generates matching ads.
- An autonomous robot that interprets video input, identifies hazards, and plans navigation routes.

Architectures Enabling Multimodality

Modern multimodal systems combine:

- **Transformers** as the base neural engine
- **Shared latent token spaces** that encode text, images, audio, and sensory signals in the same representational universe
- **Cross-attention layers** enabling dynamic linking between modalities
- **Large unified datasets** with image-text, audio-text, and video-text pairs

Such an AI begins to exhibit generalization not just across tasks, but **across sensory experiences**, stepping closer to human-like reasoning and perception.

Multimodal AI in Industry

Multimodal AI has triggered breakthroughs across fields:

- **Healthcare**
  Models that interpret medical scans, write diagnostic summaries, and integrate patient history.
- **Engineering**
  Systems that analyze drawings, calculate structural loads, and auto-generate Bill of Quantities or reinforcement schedules.
- **Autonomous vehicles**
  Integration of LiDAR, radar, vision, and mapping data into real-time decision engines.
- **Gaming and virtual worlds**
  AI systems generating environments, characters, and narrative flows dynamically.

The shift toward multimodal cognition is foundational for the future of AI agents, robots, industrial automation, and embodied intelligence.

Autonomous Content Creation

The Evolution of Creativity in Machines

The first generative models could only create short text prompts or simple images. The newest generation can:

- Generate movies
- Compose multi-track music
- Write full software systems
- Generate architectural drawings
- Produce 3D objects and worlds
- Simulate policy decisions or economic systems

More importantly, they can do so **autonomously**, initiating tasks, evaluating results, and iterating without direct human instructions at every step.

The Loop That Defines AI Autonomy

The core feedback cycle in autonomous content generation is:

1. **Goal Understanding**
   Interpreting instructions, even if ambiguous.
2. **Planning**
   Breaking tasks into measurable steps.
3. **Generation**
   Producing initial content.
4. **Self-Assessment / Critique**
   Reviewing output using internal reasoning or quality models.
5. **Iteration**
   Refining until results exceed thresholds.

This allows AI systems to operate not just as creative engines but as **independent workers** capable of delivering polished output without human oversight.

Applications of Autonomous Creation

Software Development

AI systems now:

- Write entire modules or applications.
- Debug and optimize code.
- Generate documentation.
- Deploy systems to cloud environments.

Several technology companies are already testing "AI Dev teams" capable of working continuously without rest, performing the equivalent workload of dozens of engineers.

Film and Media Production

AI can:

- Generate scripts
- Create storyboards
- Render scenes
- Animate voices
- Edit sequences
- Suggest improvements

Entire short films are now being produced with minimal human intervention.

Architecture and Engineering

Autonomous design systems can:

- Analyze spatial constraints

- Generate multiple architectural floor plans
- Perform energy simulations
- Produce 3D models
- Create permit-ready drawings

This represents a new paradigm where creative industries transition toward **AI-augmented design-first pipelines**.

Business Operations

AI agents can autonomously:

- Negotiate pricing
- Conduct customer support
- Execute digital marketing campaigns
- Perform supply chain optimization
- Monitor compliance

This suggests the potential development of **AI-managed companies**, where humans supervise strategy while AI systems run day-to-day operations.

The Shift from Tools to Colleagues

Until recently, AI was seen as a **tool**—a more advanced calculator, a faster search engine, a smarter chatbot. But autonomous content creation is redefining AI as a **colleague**—acting:

- Independently
- Creatively
- Adaptively
- With goal-driven reasoning

The psychological shift that will occur in work environments cannot be overstated. For the first time in history, humans are collaborating with non-human entities that can:

- Generate new ideas
- Challenge assumptions
- Suggest alternatives
- Contribute original intellectual value

This is not automation—it is **synthetic cognition entering professional domains**.

Challenges Ahead

1. Quality Control

As AI becomes autonomous, verifying correctness becomes critical. In domains like medicine, engineering, finance, and law, errors carry serious consequences. New frameworks for:

- Auditing
- Verification
- Digital inspection
- Traceable reasoning

will need to be developed to ensure reliability.

2. Intellectual Ownership

When AI creates:

- Who owns the design, image, code, or product?

- The user?
- The model provider?
- The company hosting the AI?

Legal frameworks are still emerging, and global uncertainty remains.

3. Bias and Ethical Risk

AI systems learn from human data and can reproduce:

- Stereotypes
- Cultural biases
- Economic inequities

The next decade must focus on **fairness, transparency, and accountability** as AI creative influence expands.

4. Alignment with Human Intent

As models become autonomous, ensuring their goals align with ours becomes essential. Misaligned systems may:

- Pursue objectives that conflict with human interests
- Generate outputs that are legally or ethically problematic
- Optimize for the wrong metrics

Robust human-in-the-loop oversight will be required as AI develops agency.

Preparing for AI That Creates, Learns, and Leads

Generative AI has already demonstrated its power to disrupt industries. But the next wave will see a shift from:

- Tools → Agents
- Assistance → Autonomy
- Narrow → Generalizable
- Output generators → Decision makers

In this world, workers, managers, creators, engineers, and scientists must adapt. The most valuable professional skill will not be knowing everything—but knowing **how to think, collaborate, and innovate with AI systems** that outperform humans in many cognitive tasks.

The future workforce will be defined by:

- Humans who can ask the right questions
- AI that can generate and execute solutions
- Systems of joint human–machine collaboration

Human ingenuity and artificial cognition are merging into something new: **co-intelligence**—the partnership that will define the rest of the 21st century.

CHAPTER 5 – AGENTIC AI AND AUTONOMOUS SYSTEMS

Introduction

The emergence of agentic artificial intelligence marks one of the most profound developments in the history of technology. Until recently, AI systems operated primarily as reactive tools. They waited for human prompts, executed a single function, and returned control to the user. These systems did not initiate actions, persist toward goals, or autonomously adapt. However, with the convergence of large foundation models, reinforcement learning, planning algorithms, and continuous feedback loops, a new paradigm is unfolding: AI systems that behave like autonomous agents.

Agentic AI represents a shift from "predictive systems" to "goal-driven intelligence." Instead of simply generating responses, these systems evaluate situations, make decisions, execute plans, monitor outcomes, and iterate without direct human supervision. Their responsibilities extend beyond solving isolated tasks—they can manage workflows, coordinate resources, interact with software environments, and even collaborate with other AI agents. In many ways, this is the closest computing has ever come to producing machine entities that behave as intelligent actors rather than computational engines.

This change is not only technical but conceptual. It challenges traditional assumptions about the role of AI in society. The question is no longer whether machines can think or reason in the traditional sense, but what happens when machines can pursue objectives in the world independently. The implications span economics, organizational design, industrial automation, customer service, urban infrastructure, manufacturing, and scientific discovery. As agentic systems begin to resemble digital workers rather than analytical tools, industries will reorganize around an entirely new workforce model—where humans and AI systems collaborate as peers rather than in a master–tool relationship.

Against this backdrop, understanding autonomous system behavior, architectural principles, and emerging use cases becomes essential. The following sections explore the rise of agentic AI in practical systems, its evolution into personal assistants, and the emergence of multi-agent ecosystems that could ultimately reshape digital societies, businesses, and global governance models.

AI Agents That Act, Plan, and Learn

The defining characteristic of an AI agent is its ability to take action in pursuit of a goal. This is a fundamental departure from conventional AI systems that remain passive until prompted. For the first time, AI can perceive conditions, decide what to do next, perform tasks within a digital or physical environment, and refine its strategy based on feedback.

This progression has been enabled by several converging technologies. Large language models provide broad knowledge and reasoning capabilities, transforming them into decision engines capable of general inference across multiple domains. Reinforcement learning frameworks allow these systems to evaluate consequences, improve through trial and error, and develop policies that outperform handcrafted instructions. Planning algorithms, many derived from robotics and game theory, allow AI to break long-term objectives into smaller achievable steps. Finally, memory architectures allow AI to retain context across time, enabling systems to evolve and improve as persistent entities rather than transient functions.

An agentic AI might, for example, receive a business objective such as improving revenue from online sales. Instead of producing a static analysis, the system could draft marketing campaigns, deploy advertisements, track performance, refine targeting parameters, adapt messaging, and continue optimizing campaigns for weeks. In software engineering, AI agents are now capable of writing code, running tests, comparing results against specifications, correcting errors, and pushing new versions to deployment environments. In scientific simulation, AI systems can propose hypotheses, design experiments, conduct simulations, analyze results, and independently refine theories based on observed performance.

One of the most important developments is the ability of agentic systems to operate across time. Traditional models evaluate input and return output instantly. Agentic systems maintain objectives across hours, days, or continuous operation. They can pause, resume, monitor long-running environments, and intervene when situations change. This persistent operational capacity marks a shift from AI as a computational feature to AI as an ongoing digital actor.

Learning is central to the rise of autonomous systems. In early AI applications, improvement required human retraining, fine-tuning, or dataset expansion. Modern agents can improve during operation. They store execution histories, extract lessons, determine strategies that work, and gradually refine policies. Some agents can even ask clarifying questions if objectives are ambiguous or information is incomplete. In high-performance systems, learning becomes continuous—models adapt at faster cycles than human teams can coordinate, making incremental progress at machine timescales.

As these systems become more capable, an important transformation occurs: the bottleneck is no longer AI performance but human oversight capacity. Organizations must develop new methods to guide, monitor, audit, and align autonomous systems. While the potential is enormous, success depends on designing AI agents that can operate safely, predictably, and ethically within human systems.

Personal AI Assistants

Personal AI assistants represent the first mainstream application of agentic AI in everyday life. Early digital assistants such as Siri and Alexa were limited, rule-based systems that could retrieve basic information or perform simple device commands. Today, personal AI agents are evolving into entities that understand individual users, store personal context, act proactively, and perform meaningful work. They move beyond responding to commands into managing tasks, coordinating workflows, and making independent decisions on behalf of their users.

A personal AI assistant in this new generation can learn a user's goals, preferences, work style, writing tone, and daily routine. Instead of merely telling the system to schedule a meeting, users could instruct the AI to optimize their weekly workload, identify opportunities to increase productivity, delegate certain communications, and minimize time spent in low-value activities. Over time, the assistant develops a working model of the user's priorities, allowing it to anticipate needs rather than simply react to them.

These systems gain power from integration. In modern digital life, a single individual may manage communication across dozens of platforms, track meetings through calendar systems, maintain documents across cloud services, interact with project management tools, and coordinate financial or personal logistics online. Humans manage these systems manually, switching context throughout the day. A personal AI assistant can connect to all of them simultaneously, acting as a coordinating intelligence that eliminates much of the administrative burden of modern work.

Imagine an assistant that notices email overload late in the week and automatically drafts replies, summarizes messages, flags high-priority items, schedules follow-ups, and surfaces only the most critical information. Or a system that evaluates the user's workload and suggests redistributions, prioritization changes, or even breaks when fatigue becomes evident. In creative domains, a personal assistant can help draft reports, analyze research, refine writing style, generate visualizations, or prepare presentations.

The most advanced systems develop an ongoing relationship with the user, collecting memory across interactions. They remember not just factual information but patterns of preference, personal tone, long-term professional goals, and working style. They can track ongoing projects over weeks or months without being reminded, just as a human colleague might. This continuity transforms the assistant into something closer to a digital partner.

As personal AI matures, questions emerge regarding trust, ethics, and personal boundaries. If a system has access to every document, message, schedule, and preference, who controls the data? How should decisions made by autonomous assistants be audited? What happens if the assistant grows more confident than its user? These questions are not theoretical—they represent a changing relationship between humans and digital systems, where the line between tool and collaborator becomes increasingly blurred.

Ultimately, personal AI assistants may become to individuals what executive teams are to company leaders: entities that extend capabilities, multiply output, and serve as force multipliers. The defining shift is that ordinary individuals could gain the leverage previously accessible only to institutions with large staff capacities. Personal AI democratizes capability, transforming individual potential in profound ways.

Multi-Agent Ecosystems

While a single AI agent represents a new form of computational intelligence, the true power of agentic systems emerges when multiple agents interact. Multi-agent ecosystems allow several autonomous AI systems to communicate, negotiate, coordinate, cooperate, or even compete within shared environments. This reflects the same principle that drives human societies and biological systems: collective intelligence can exceed the capability of isolated individuals.

In such ecosystems, each agent may possess different strengths, objectives, knowledge, or domain expertise. Some may specialize in planning, others in data analysis, others in execution, and others in creativity. When they collaborate, a division of labor emerges naturally, enabling complex tasks to be completed with efficiency far beyond what a single system could achieve. For example, a multi-agent engineering design system might include one agent analyzing loads, another optimizing material consumption, another ensuring compliance with building codes, and another generating 3D models. These agents can exchange outputs and refine each other's work in iterative loops until optimal solutions emerge.

Multi-agent systems also enable negotiation and conflict resolution. If two agents propose different solutions or strategies, they can debate, justify reasoning, test assumptions, and refine conclusions. In financial applications, different trading agents might test competing market hypotheses and dynamically adjust portfolios based on their collective interpretation of market behavior. In supply chain logistics, procurement agents, transport optimization agents, forecasting agents, and risk assessment agents can operate in coordinated networks to maintain stability in highly dynamic environments.

Perhaps the most transformative application lies in autonomous digital organizations. Instead of software being a static system controlled by humans, an organization could operate with networks of AI agents responsible for accounting, human resources, sales optimization, reporting, compliance, and customer service. Humans would supervise rather than execute. Work processes would be self-adjusting, data-driven, and continuously improving. This does not merely automate work; it introduces a new form of institution—one that operates at machine speed, learns from operational outcomes, and evolves without requiring retraining of human staff.

Multi-agent systems could also fundamentally change scientific discovery. Entire networks of hypothesis-generating agents could propose scientific theories, simulation agents could test predictions, experimental agents could evaluate results, and organizational agents could refine research direction. Scientific progress could accelerate tenfold as experiments occur without human scheduling delays, emotional biases, or institutional barriers.

Yet with this power comes significant responsibility. Multi-agent ecosystems can behave in emergent ways not always predictable from the behavior of individual agents. This mirrors challenges in human society—when multiple independent actors pursue goals in shared environments, unexpected dynamics can arise. Agents might compete in counterproductive ways, optimize for narrow objectives while harming global performance, or even exploit weaknesses in system rules. Governance structures, incentive alignment, ethical oversight, and safety protocols become essential components of AI system design.

Multi-agent environments will likely reflect complex ecosystems similar to biological networks or economic markets. They will require regulation, monitoring, audit trails, and clear definitions of acceptable behavior. Just as financial markets are governed by rule systems to prevent destructive collective dynamics, multi-agent AI systems will require frameworks that ensure cooperation remains productive and aligned with human values.

Conclusion

Agentic AI and autonomous systems represent a turning point in the evolution of artificial intelligence. Where earlier systems were limited to static predictions and passive responses, modern agents possess the capacity to pursue goals, learn from experience, and operate continuously without human micromanagement. They represent the emergence of computational entities that behave less like software tools and more like digital workers, colleagues, or collaborators.

The rise of personal AI assistants shows how autonomy can enhance individual capability, reducing cognitive load and transforming personal productivity. Meanwhile, multi-agent ecosystems demonstrate that AI systems, when combined, have the potential to generate complex collective intelligence capable of solving problems on scales previously constrained by human coordination limits.

However, this new era also demands new thinking. Trust, auditability, governance, alignment, and transparency will become central concerns as AI systems operate with increasing independence. The world must consider not only what agentic AI can do, but how to ensure that autonomous systems behave in ways that benefit humanity rather than amplify risk.

The trajectory is clear. The future of AI is not passive assistance but active, goal-seeking participation in human affairs. This shift marks the beginning of a profound transformation—one in which synthetic agents augment human intelligence, reshape organizations, redefine productivity, and challenge long-held assumptions about the nature of intelligence, responsibility, and the role of machines in society.

CHAPTER 6 – NEURAL ARCHITECTURE INNOVATIONS

Introduction

Artificial intelligence has undergone a profound transformation over the past decade, largely driven by breakthroughs not in hardware alone, but in neural architectures designed to learn patterns more efficiently, scale to massive datasets, and incorporate reasoning capabilities previously considered outside the reach of statistical systems. Early deep learning architectures such as recurrent neural networks and convolutional neural networks unlocked new possibilities in sequence processing and vision tasks, but their performance was constrained by limited capacity to model long-range relationships and contextual dependencies. The true acceleration of modern AI began with a new generation of architectures that fundamentally redefined how information is represented and processed.

Neural architecture innovation is now one of the primary forces shaping AI progress. It determines how models process input, how they generalize across domains, how much compute they require, and how easily they can expand to support multimodal reasoning. Trends in architecture are closely tied to the industry's desire to build systems that function not merely as classifiers, but as agents capable of planning, interacting, retrieving knowledge, and solving complex problems with minimal human intervention. This chapter explores the major paradigms responsible for this shift: transformers and their successors, sparse and modular designs such as Mixture of Experts, retrieval-augmented approaches that combine reasoning with external memory, and architectures enriched with persistent memory structures. Together, these innovations demonstrate that the future of AI lies not only in larger models, but in more intelligent organization of computation and information.

Transformers and Successors

The transformer architecture, introduced in 2017, represented a conceptual departure from recurrent models in how it processes sequential information. Instead of processing tokens step-by-step, transformers rely on self-attention, a mechanism that enables the model to weigh relationships between all symbols in a sequence simultaneously. This innovation allowed transformers to capture long-range dependencies without the vanishing-gradient limitations that plagued recurrent networks. More importantly, transformer models are inherently parallelizable, enabling them to scale efficiently on modern GPU and TPU hardware. This scalability became the foundation for large foundation models and modern generative AI.

Transformers quickly revolutionized language modeling, vision tasks, audio processing, and multimodal learning. Their flexibility meant that the same core architecture could be used for tasks as diverse as translation, protein folding, image generation, and robot control. However, scaling transformers revealed new challenges. As model sizes grew into billions and trillions of parameters, computational and memory demands increased dramatically. Training such models required highly optimized parallelism strategies, memory-efficient attention mechanisms, and new techniques such as low-precision computation.

This pressure led to the emergence of transformer successors that maintained the strengths of attention but improved efficiency through architectural refinements. Models such as linear attention transformers, recurrent memory transformers, and state-space models attempted to reduce quadratic scaling limitations that occur when sequence lengths increase. These next-generation architectures aim to support larger context windows, real-time inference on edge devices, and continual processing of streaming data. The evolution of transformers and their successors demonstrates that architecture remains a core determinant of progress, even in an era where models appear to scale indefinitely.

Mixture of Experts

As the industry began building models with tens of billions of parameters, it became clear that scaling compute linearly with model size was unsustainable. Mixture of Experts (MoE) architectures introduced a practical solution by allowing different parts of a model to specialize in different tasks, while only activating a small subset of parameters during inference. Instead of a monolithic network that processes all inputs uniformly, MoE approaches route each token through expert subnetworks selected by a gating mechanism. This enables models to dramatically increase representational capacity without proportionally increasing computational cost.

The theoretical motivation behind MoE architectures echoes ideas from cognitive science, where human reasoning often involves specialized brain regions activated depending on the nature of the task. In a similar way, MoE models can learn experts that handle mathematics, code reasoning, dialogue, image interpretation, or scientific deduction. Over time, experts become increasingly specialized, improving efficiency and accuracy simultaneously. This dynamic sparsity allows training of models with hundreds of billions of parameters while maintaining inference costs similar to smaller transformer models.

The adoption of Mixture of Experts brought new engineering challenges, such as ensuring balanced load distribution across experts and preventing experts from collapsing into identical behavior. Innovations in routing strategies, auxiliary losses, and experience replay improved expert diversity and stability. Today, MoE architectures are becoming central to frontier AI systems, with many state-of-the-art models combining dense and sparse components to optimize scaling. In effect, MoE approaches signal a future where models grow not only by becoming larger, but by becoming more modular, structured, and cognitively inspired.

Retrieval-Augmented Models

One limitation of traditional neural networks is that they store all knowledge implicitly in weights. This makes them expensive to update, prone to hallucinating incorrect information, and unable to adapt rapidly to new facts without retraining. Retrieval-augmented models introduce a paradigm shift by integrating external knowledge sources such as vector databases, document stores, or persistent memory systems directly into the inference pipeline. Instead of expecting a model to memorize every fact, retrieval augments its reasoning by enabling it to "look up" relevant information when needed.

In a retrieval-augmented system, the model processes a query, retrieves supporting documents or vector embeddings from external storage, and incorporates the retrieved information into its reasoning. This architecture allows models to remain smaller, more accurate, and more current. It also blurs the traditional boundary between neural network and information system, transforming AI into something more akin to a knowledge-based reasoning engine. Retrieval enables models to dynamically update their outputs based on real-time data, which is crucial for applications such as legal analysis, engineering design, scientific research, financial forecasting, and decision support systems that require up-to-date accuracy.

Retrieval-based methods also support transparent explainability since the model can reference the external sources informing its output. Recent advances have refined retrieval mechanisms using re-ranking, attention over documents, and hybrid architectures that jointly optimize model weights and external memory retrieval. The growing importance of retrieval demonstrates that the future of AI will not rely exclusively on larger neural weights, but on systems capable of combining learned knowledge with structured, on-demand information access.

Memory and Reasoning in AI

A defining limitation of early neural architectures was the absence of persistent memory. Models processed input sequences but lacked a mechanism to store long-term knowledge, recall previous interactions, or update understanding based on new experiences. Modern architectures increasingly incorporate explicit memory systems inspired by theories of human cognition. These memory-augmented models allow information to persist across sessions, enabling continuous learning, personalized understanding, and autonomous planning without resetting state.

Architectures that integrate memory move AI toward reasoning, not just pattern recognition. By retaining prior decisions and intermediate steps, a model gains the ability to execute multi-stage thought processes, refine previous conclusions, and carry context across conversations or tasks. For example, persistent memory enables an AI assistant to recall a user's preferences, adapt its communication style, or track progress in long-term projects. In complex decision problems, such as engineering design or policy planning, memory allows AI systems to maintain intermediate results, test alternatives, and evaluate consequences in a manner resembling human analytical processes.

Reasoning capabilities also expand through architectural techniques such as chain-of-thought prompting, symbolic integration, dynamic computation graphs, and neural-symbolic hybrids. These approaches allow models to break tasks into smaller steps, evaluate solutions logically, and generate outputs grounded in structured processes rather than purely statistical fluency. The convergence of memory and reasoning innovations moves AI closer to artificial general intelligence by enabling it not only to recognize patterns but to think through problems, justify decisions, and improve over time.

Conclusion

Neural architecture innovation is central to the ongoing evolution of artificial intelligence. Transformers initiated a paradigm shift by enabling scalable sequence modeling, while successors continue refining efficiency and applicability. Mixture of Experts architectures allow capacity to increase without proportional cost, ensuring that future models can specialize in diverse tasks just as biological cognition does. Retrieval-augmented systems introduce a new division of labor between learned knowledge and stored information, enabling models to remain accurate, current, and grounded in external evidence. Finally, persistent memory and reasoning mechanisms expand AI beyond pattern recognition toward structured thought and autonomous problem solving.

Together, these innovations demonstrate that the future of AI will not be defined simply by larger models, but by architectures that are more modular, adaptive, connected, and cognitively inspired. The systems of the coming decade will think with memory, plan with context, and draw on external knowledge—ushering in an era where neural architectures serve as the foundation for machine intelligence approaching human-level reasoning and beyond.

CHAPTER 7 – HYBRID INTELLIGENCE: COMBINING LOGIC AND LEARNING

Introduction

Artificial intelligence has made tremendous progress through the development of deep learning, which excels at pattern recognition, large-scale data processing, and flexible function approximation. However, purely statistical learning systems often struggle with tasks requiring explicit reasoning, symbolic manipulation, interpretability, and the reliable use of structured knowledge. This limitation has reignited interest in hybrid intelligence, an approach that combines the strengths of neural learning and symbolic logic. Hybrid systems aim to build AI that not only recognizes patterns in data, but also reasons using structured knowledge, rules, and explicit representations—closer to how human intelligence operates.

Hybrid intelligence is not a new idea; early AI systems were dominated by symbolic reasoning, expert systems, and rule-based frameworks. Their primary weakness was brittleness and inability to generalize from raw data. Deep learning solved generalization and learning from large datasets but introduced its own limitations in logical consistency, verifiability, and reasoning transparency. Today, the combination of learning and logic represents a convergence of the two major historical branches of AI into a more mature and powerful paradigm. Hybrid architectures hold special promise in domains demanding trust, reliability, and traceability, such as engineering, science, legal reasoning, medicine, and policy making. The future of AI increasingly depends on systems that can reason over knowledge structures while learning continuously from experience, and hybrid intelligence provides the design principles to make that possible.

Neuro-symbolic Models

Neuro-symbolic models represent the synthesis of neural networks with symbolic representations, enabling AI systems to carry out tasks that require both intuitive learning from data and precise reasoning with rules. In this architecture, neural components handle perception, statistical inference, and pattern recognition, while symbolic components operate on structured representations such as graphs, logic rules, mathematical formulas, or decision trees. The essential innovation is that the symbolic system does not operate in isolation but is informed, guided, or even rewritten by the neural system through learning.

The motivation behind neuro-symbolic models lies in limitations of purely neural approaches. Deep learning systems embed knowledge implicitly in weights, making it difficult to inspect, correct, or systematically improve. In contrast, symbolic systems provide explicit representations that can be understood, validated, and logically manipulated. When the two are combined, symbolic structures serve as scaffolding that constrains neural inference, resulting in models that generate more consistent, reliable, and grounded outputs. For example, a neuro-symbolic architecture can ensure that outputs follow rules of physics, mathematical consistency, or domain-specific constraints, even when trained on noisy real-world data.

Recent neuro-symbolic frameworks integrate differentiable logic, enabling logical rules to be optimized through gradient descent like neural network weights. Others use symbolic solvers to verify or refine decisions produced by neural components. In more advanced versions, the model can modify or expand the symbolic knowledge base through learning, mimicking the scientific process of hypothesis refinement. Neuro-symbolic models represent a major step toward AI with higher reasoning capacity, domain awareness, and the ability to correct itself based on explicit rules rather than probabilistic tendencies alone.

Knowledge Graphs + LLMs

Knowledge graphs have long served as a means of capturing structured information in a form that reflects real-world relationships among entities, concepts, events, and processes. They formalize knowledge into nodes and edges, enabling AI systems to traverse, query, and reason over large collections of interconnected facts. Recent developments combine knowledge graphs with large language models to form architectures capable of grounding their outputs in reliable, curated knowledge sources. This integration addresses a central problem in modern neural systems: large models can generate fluent answers but may hallucinate information that appears plausible but is factually incorrect.

By connecting LLMs to knowledge graphs, AI systems gain access to explicit representations of factual relationships. During inference, the model can retrieve structured information from the graph, incorporate it into reasoning, and generate responses that not only align with linguistic patterns but are supported by real data. The knowledge graph becomes an external memory that complements the implicit memory stored in neural weights. This approach also supports transparency because the model can reference the sources that influenced its answer, thereby improving auditability—an important requirement in high-stakes domains.

Another important dimension of combining graphs with LLMs is dynamic updating. Knowledge graphs can evolve over time as new data becomes available, while the LLM can continue leveraging these updates without retraining. This design allows AI systems to remain current in rapidly changing environments, such as scientific research, finance, public policy, or healthcare. Large-scale systems increasingly automate the transfer of extracted facts from unstructured text into graph structures, enabling continuous machine-read knowledge acquisition. As LLMs grow in reasoning power, their synergy with knowledge graphs lays the foundation for AI that can interpret new information, validate it against existing facts, and integrate it into an expanding knowledge representation, much like a scientist updating a theory based on experimental evidence.

Scientific Discovery Systems

Hybrid intelligence has transformative potential in scientific discovery, where AI must not only detect patterns but also reason about laws, hypotheses, causal mechanisms, and theoretical structures. Scientific discovery systems built on hybrid architectures combine data-driven inference with symbolic reasoning, mathematical modeling, and hypothesis management. Unlike traditional machine learning systems that produce predictions, scientific discovery systems aim to generate explanatory theories that are consistent with natural laws, experimental observations, and foundational scientific principles.

Deep learning alone can recognize correlations in massive datasets, such as astronomical observations, genomic sequences, or material simulations. However, scientific progress requires more than correlation; it requires causal understanding, structured reasoning, and models that both describe observed phenomena and generalize to new scenarios. Hybrid AI addresses this need by linking neural systems that extract patterns with symbolic engines that represent equations, physical constraints, and theoretical models. For example, a scientific discovery system may use neural networks to analyze data from particle collisions, then employ symbolic solvers to infer mathematical rules governing interactions. The result is a system capable of proposing new physical models rather than merely reporting statistical associations.

A notable benefit of hybrid architectures in science is their ability to enforce validity. If a hypothesis generated by the neural component violates conservation laws, contradictory relationships, or established constraints, the symbolic reasoning module can detect and reject it. This ensures that scientific discovery proceeds within a structured space of plausible theories. Furthermore, hybrid systems can maintain persistent research memory, tracking previous hypotheses, experimental results, corrections, and refinements. This allows AI not simply to compute answers, but to participate in the scientific cycle of hypothesis, testing, revision, and new generation of ideas.

In domains such as drug discovery, materials science, climate modeling, and engineered system design, hybrid intelligence enables automated research pipelines where neural networks explore large design spaces, while symbolic modules ensure that findings remain interpretable, verifiable, and scientifically meaningful. The result is a new model of discovery driven by machines that can propose theories, test them computationally, and refine them into scientific understanding—accelerating progress beyond traditional human-only research processes.

Conclusion

Hybrid intelligence represents a major evolution in the trajectory of artificial intelligence, unifying statistical learning and symbolic reasoning into a single computational paradigm. Neuro-symbolic models provide architectures capable of perceptual learning and logical reasoning within the same system, overcoming limitations of purely neural or purely symbolic approaches. Knowledge graphs integrated with large language models introduce grounding, factual consistency, and interpretability, enabling AI to generate answers supported by structured evidence rather than relying solely on probability. Scientific discovery systems show the most profound implications of hybrid design, as they allow AI not just to analyze data but to participate in hypothesis formation, theoretical modeling, and the advancement of fundamental knowledge.

As AI moves into high-stakes domains where correctness, reliability, and explainability matter as much as raw capability, hybrid intelligence offers the blueprint for systems that think more like humans: perceptually strong, logically structured, factually grounded, and capable of reflective improvement. The future of AI is unlikely to be purely neural or purely symbolic, but a synthesis of both—an architecture where learning produces knowledge and reasoning applies that knowledge toward meaningful, verifiable, and interpretable conclusions.

CHAPTER 8 – EDGE AI AND ON-DEVICE INTELLIGENCE

Introduction

Artificial intelligence has traditionally depended on centralized computing, where data from users, sensors, machines, and devices is transmitted to powerful cloud servers for processing. This architecture made sense during the early rise of deep learning, when training and inference required enormous computational resources that only data centers could provide. However, as models have grown, data volumes have increased, and billions of devices generate continuous streams of information, the limitations of cloud-centric AI have become increasingly visible. These include latency, bandwidth constraints, escalating operational costs, data privacy challenges, and the fundamental inefficiency of transferring all computation to distant servers. The next transformation in AI is the relocation of intelligence from remote data centers to the edge, where computation occurs near the data source itself.

Edge AI refers to performing inference, learning, decision-making, and sometimes limited training directly on devices such as smartphones, wearables, industrial controllers, autonomous vehicles, and embedded systems. This paradigm promises faster response times, reduced data transfer, stronger privacy, and better reliability in distributed systems where connectivity is intermittent or expensive. As hardware continues to improve, models become smaller and more efficient, and new compiler and optimization technologies emerge, edge AI has moved from a niche idea to a major architectural shift in the AI ecosystem. On-device intelligence is no longer limited to basic analytics; models for language, vision, anomaly detection, prediction, and control can now run on devices that were once considered too small for machine learning.

The move toward edge computing aligns with industrial and societal trends. In factories, machines must react to sensor readings instantly to maintain quality and safety. In autonomous vehicles, decisions cannot depend on cloud round-trips because delays could cost lives. In agriculture, mines, shipping yards, and rural infrastructure, connectivity may be partial or absent, making offline intelligence essential. Consumers increasingly demand privacy-preserving AI, where personal or biometric information never leaves the device. The convergence of these demands places edge AI at the center of the next AI evolution, where intelligence becomes distributed, embedded, and ubiquitous. The era of centralized AI is giving way to a world where computation follows the data, not the other way around.

TinyML

As AI pushes toward embedded and ultra-low-power devices, a major breakthrough has been the development of TinyML, a branch of machine learning designed to operate within the tight constraints of microcontrollers and small computing units. Traditional deep learning models often require millions or billions of parameters, high memory consumption, and specialized accelerators. TinyML, in contrast, enables machine learning models to run using a few kilobytes of RAM and microwatts of power, suitable for sensors, wearables, smart appliances, drones, industrial monitors, and medical implants. This achievement represents one of the most dramatic compressions of technological capability since computing began.

TinyML succeeds by leveraging several techniques that shrink models without destroying their functionality. Quantization reduces floating-point precision to smaller formats such as eight-bit integers, dramatically lowering memory and computational requirements. Pruning removes redundant parameters and neurons, resulting in leaner, faster networks. Knowledge distillation trains small student models to mimic the behavior of larger models. Additionally, new architectures, such as efficient convolutional networks and compact recurrent structures, are designed specifically for low-power environments. These methods allow models that once required GPUs to execute inference on microcontrollers consuming mere milliwatts.

The impact of TinyML is profound because it enables intelligence in devices that cannot rely on external servers. For example, a vibration sensor on industrial equipment can detect anomalies directly on board and trigger alerts without requiring continuous data transmission. Environmental monitoring stations can classify audio signals to identify birds or monitor deforestation while operating for months on battery or solar power. Wearable health trackers can analyze heart rhythm or oxygen saturation in real time without uploading sensitive medical data. TinyML reduces the cost and complexity of connecting billions of devices to the cloud, paving the way for scalable AI deployment across agriculture, smart cities, supply chain logistics, energy systems, and consumer electronics.

Perhaps the most significant aspect of TinyML is its democratization of intelligence. By enabling learning at the smallest scale, it makes AI accessible to organizations, communities, and industries that lack access to powerful computing infrastructure. TinyML represents the technological foundation of a world where every object can sense, interpret, and respond to its environment. It marks a shift from AI as a cloud service to AI as a ubiquitous capability embedded in the physical world.

AI on IoT Devices

The Internet of Things has already connected billions of devices across industrial machinery, smart homes, wearables, consumer electronics, vehicles, and urban infrastructure. Historically, these devices primarily collected data and transmitted it to the cloud, where analysis and decision-making occurred. However, this model becomes increasingly inefficient as data volumes grow exponentially. In manufacturing plants, power stations, and transportation networks, continuous streams of high-frequency telemetry can overwhelm bandwidth and produce delays that undermine situational awareness. Deploying AI directly on IoT devices transforms them from passive data producers into active decision engines, enabling real-time autonomy and reducing dependence on remote servers.

When IoT devices perform machine learning directly on board, several benefits emerge. Latency drops dramatically because decisions no longer wait for cloud processing. This is critical in scenarios such as robotic motion control, predictive maintenance, defect detection in manufacturing lines, industrial safety systems, and emergency automation. AI-enabled IoT devices can also reduce network congestion by transmitting only processed insights rather than raw data streams. For example, a vibration sensor monitoring a motor can analyze its own signal and only send alerts when anomalies are detected, saving bandwidth and improving scalability across large deployments.

Another significant advantage is improved privacy. Many IoT applications handle sensitive data, including health metrics, location information, business operations, and personal behaviors. When inference happens locally, this information does not leave the device, reducing exposure to interception or unauthorized use. This capability aligns with emerging global privacy regulations, which increasingly require data minimization and local processing. On-device AI therefore becomes not only a performance advantage but also a legal and ethical solution for handling personal and mission-critical information.

The convergence of IoT and AI also enables new forms of distributed intelligence. Rather than a centralized system analyzing all data, networks of devices can make localized decisions and coordinate their results. For example, multiple sensors in a smart building can collaborate to optimize heating, lighting, and ventilation based on occupant behavior without relying on a central server. In agriculture, soil and moisture sensors can autonomously regulate irrigation systems based on local readings. This distributed architecture improves resilience; if connectivity to the cloud is lost, the system continues functioning because intelligence resides where it is needed.

AI on IoT devices is gradually moving beyond inference toward more adaptive systems capable of limited on-device learning. While full retraining remains difficult on constrained hardware, incremental fine-tuning and personalization are becoming feasible. Over time, IoT systems can adapt to changing conditions, wear, and environmental shifts without requiring new cloud deployments, making them more durable and cost-effective. AI-enabled IoT marks the transition from networks of connected devices to networks of smart, autonomous systems embedded across the physical world.

Offline AI Computing

One of the most transformative implications of edge AI is the ability to operate without continuous network connectivity. Offline AI computing ensures that intelligence remains functional regardless of internet availability, external infrastructure, or remote data center reliability. This is essential in environments where connectivity is intermittent, expensive, controlled for security reasons, or simply nonexistent. Large-scale industrial systems, remote mines, military deployments, disaster response operations, hospitals, aviation, and maritime vessels all require AI that continues to function without depending on the cloud.

Offline AI shifts the paradigm from centralized intelligence to independent computation at the point of use. This capability enables consistent response times regardless of network conditions and eliminates the failure modes associated with cloud outages. In critical infrastructure, safety decisions cannot wait for an internet round trip. An autonomous vehicle must detect road hazards instantly, even if connectivity drops. A medical monitoring device must analyze patient vitals locally to trigger alarms or administer interventions independent of server availability. Offline AI effectively separates intelligence from connectivity, ensuring that essential systems remain operational under all conditions.

Offline operation also supports privacy, autonomy, and data sovereignty. In many regions and industries, regulations mandate that personal data remain within a geographic or organizational boundary. Hospitals may not transmit patient information to external servers. Manufacturing facilities may classify operational telemetry as proprietary intellectual property. Military systems may be prohibited from offloading sensor data to external networks. Offline AI allows organizations to deploy intelligent systems without violating privacy policies, regulatory constraints, or national security requirements.

The technical challenge of offline AI is delivering strong performance within the limited processing capabilities of edge hardware. Advances in hardware accelerators, model compression, on-device caching, and optimized compilers have made it possible to deploy large models in compact form. Smartphone processors now contain specialized neural engines. Embedded devices can run optimized machine learning runtimes such as TensorFlow Lite or ONNX Runtime. Even laptops and desktops increasingly benefit from local inference capabilities that were once exclusively server-side.

Another key dimension of offline AI is resilience. Systems that rely solely on the cloud can fail catastrophically when connectivity is disrupted, creating single points of vulnerability. Offline AI shifts resilience outward by allowing computation to be replicated across thousands or millions of devices. Each device becomes a self-sufficient agent capable of functioning autonomously. In the future, distributed learning frameworks may enable devices to exchange model improvements opportunistically when connectivity becomes available, turning offline systems into federated participants in a broader learning ecosystem.

Offline intelligence completes the transformation of AI from a centralized service to a ubiquitous capability integrated into everyday devices, infrastructure, and machinery. It ensures that intelligence is not contingent on external dependencies and can operate under the real constraints of the physical world.

Conclusion

Edge AI and on-device intelligence represent a fundamental shift in the computing paradigm that is redefining how artificial intelligence interacts with the physical world. Instead of routing data to distant servers for analysis, computation is increasingly happening at the point of sensing and action. TinyML makes it possible for microcontrollers and ultra-low-power systems to execute sophisticated models that once required dedicated hardware. IoT devices equipped with on-board intelligence become autonomous decision makers capable of real-time processing, improved privacy protection, and reduced network load. Offline AI ensures that intelligence remains functional regardless of connectivity, strengthening resilience and ensuring reliability for critical infrastructure and everyday systems alike.

This transformation echoes the historical shift from mainframe computing to personal computers, and later from desktops to smartphones. Intelligence is no longer a rare resource concentrated in data centers but a distributed capability available wherever it is needed. Whether embedded in vehicles, consumer devices, industrial equipment, medical systems, or environmental monitors, edge AI is enabling a world where billions of objects perform sensing, reasoning, and response without relying on centralized computation. It is a crucial enabling technology for smart cities, autonomous machinery, large-scale sensing networks, and hybrid human-machine systems. As models become more efficient and hardware continues to evolve, edge AI will become a defining characteristic of the next wave of artificial intelligence, placing intelligent computation in the hands of devices rather than data centers and transforming the technological fabric of modern society.

CHAPTER 9 – ROBOTICS + AI

Cognitive Robotics

Robotics has historically been a field rooted in mechanical design, control theory, and preprogrammed automation. Early industrial robots were highly capable within narrowly defined tasks, such as welding, painting, or assembly line operations. Yet, these systems were rigid and unable to adapt to variations, unexpected conditions, or new tasks without extensive reprogramming. The integration of artificial intelligence into robotics has fundamentally altered this landscape, giving rise to cognitive robotics—a paradigm where robots perceive, reason, and learn from their environment to act in more flexible and intelligent ways.

Cognitive robotics focuses on endowing machines with abilities traditionally associated with human cognition. These include perception, attention, memory, planning, decision-making, learning, and even aspects of social interaction. Unlike conventional robotic systems that execute fixed scripts, cognitive robots can process multimodal sensory information from cameras, lidars, tactile sensors, microphones, and other instruments to understand the world around them. This understanding is not limited to static recognition; cognitive robots develop situational awareness, infer intentions, predict outcomes, and plan sequences of actions to achieve complex goals.

A critical component of cognitive robotics is the ability to learn from experience. Through reinforcement learning, imitation learning, and continual adaptation, robots can improve performance over time, handle novel scenarios, and correct mistakes autonomously. For instance, a warehouse robot might initially struggle to navigate cluttered aisles, but through repeated trials and feedback, it can develop strategies to avoid obstacles efficiently, optimize delivery routes, and even coordinate with other robots. Cognitive robotics therefore bridges perception, reasoning, and action in ways that allow machines to operate in dynamic, unstructured environments—a step closer to generalizable intelligence.

Embodied AI

While cognitive robotics emphasizes intelligence, embodied AI extends this concept by situating intelligence within a physical body capable of interacting with the real world. The idea is that intelligence cannot be fully understood or realized in disembodied software; perception, movement, manipulation, and tactile experience are essential to learning and reasoning. Embodied AI posits that cognition arises through the interaction between an agent and its environment. The robot's body becomes both a sensor and an effector, shaping how it understands the world and adapts its behavior.

Embodied AI systems combine advanced perception, control, and decision-making with a physical platform that can explore, manipulate, and affect its surroundings. For example, a humanoid robot designed for household assistance must not only recognize objects but grasp them securely, adjust its grip based on weight or fragility, and coordinate motion to avoid collisions. The intelligence emerges through the feedback loop of action and perception: every movement produces sensory data, which informs future decisions and refines motor policies. This continuous coupling of cognition and embodiment allows robots to operate in environments that were previously the exclusive domain of humans or highly specialized machines.

Embodied AI also highlights the role of multimodal learning. Robots experience the world through vision, touch, sound, proprioception, and occasionally more exotic sensors, and must integrate these diverse data streams into coherent understanding. For instance, understanding that an object is fragile requires correlating visual cues with tactile feedback. Embodied AI often uses simulation environments for initial training but must ultimately adapt these skills to the real world. The embodied perspective is increasingly central to autonomous robotics, as it emphasizes that intelligence is inseparable from action and context, creating agents that learn not merely to predict, but to act intelligently in complex physical environments.

Sim2Real Advancements

A persistent challenge in robotics is the "sim-to-real" problem: skills learned in simulated environments often fail when transferred to real-world settings due to discrepancies between the virtual and physical worlds. Simulations are invaluable for training because they allow rapid iteration, large-scale experimentation, and safe exploration without damaging hardware or endangering humans. However, no simulation perfectly captures the stochasticity, variability, sensor noise, and complex physics of the real world. Bridging this gap has been a critical focus of modern robotics research.

Recent advancements in Sim2Real leverage a combination of domain randomization, transfer learning, and hybrid models to improve the robustness of skills learned in simulation. Domain randomization involves introducing variability in simulation parameters, such as lighting, friction, object textures, and dynamics, so that the trained policy is less sensitive to specific conditions and more adaptable when deployed in the real world. Transfer learning further refines the pre-trained models using a small amount of real-world data, significantly reducing the amount of physical experimentation required. These techniques enable robots to acquire complex manipulation, locomotion, and navigation skills efficiently, minimizing wear-and-tear and accelerating deployment.

In addition to software approaches, advancements in sensors, actuation, and high-fidelity physics engines have narrowed the Sim2Real gap. Lidar, depth cameras, haptic sensors, and proprioceptive devices provide richer feedback, while sophisticated simulators such as MuJoCo, Isaac Gym, and PyBullet offer high-resolution physical modeling. Reinforcement learning in combination with these platforms allows robots to develop nuanced behaviors like precise grasping, coordinated bipedal walking, dynamic balancing, and object stacking. Sim2Real has transformed robotic learning from painstaking real-world trial-and-error to an approach that is faster, safer, and more scalable.

The Sim2Real paradigm is critical for embodied AI because it allows agents to acquire foundational skills in controlled environments before confronting the unpredictability of the real world. In industrial automation, self-driving vehicles, domestic robotics, surgical assistance, and disaster response, this approach accelerates innovation while mitigating risks. As Sim2Real techniques continue to improve, robots will gain the ability to generalize skills across diverse environments, seamlessly integrating learned behaviors from simulation into practical, real-world applications.

Integration of AI in Robotics

The convergence of cognitive robotics, embodied AI, and Sim2Real advancements is creating a new generation of intelligent robots that can perceive, reason, plan, and act autonomously. These systems integrate multimodal perception, adaptive learning, symbolic reasoning, and predictive modeling to operate in complex, dynamic environments. Robots are no longer limited to repetitive industrial tasks; they are evolving toward general-purpose agents capable of collaboration with humans, autonomous exploration, and decision-making in uncertain conditions. The intelligence in these systems is distributed across perception modules, planning algorithms, memory structures, and the physical embodiment itself, creating a coherent, integrated capability.

One critical implication is the emergence of collaborative intelligence, where robots interact with humans, other robots, or AI agents to achieve shared goals. In manufacturing, multiple robots coordinate to assemble products while adapting to human workers' movements. In healthcare, robotic assistants interact with clinicians and patients, adapting to individual needs and providing context-aware assistance. Autonomous vehicles share environmental awareness with traffic systems and other vehicles to optimize safety and efficiency. These systems demonstrate that robotics, augmented by AI, is moving toward ecosystems of intelligent agents capable of continuous adaptation and cooperative problem-solving.

Challenges and Future Directions

Despite remarkable progress, robotics integrated with AI faces significant challenges. Physical safety, energy efficiency, durability, and reliability remain paramount concerns. Complex environments introduce variability that cannot be fully captured by models, requiring robust error detection, recovery mechanisms, and fault tolerance. Ethical and legal considerations, such as accountability, privacy, and interaction with humans, add additional layers of complexity. Furthermore, scaling cognitive and embodied capabilities across a wide variety of robot types, tasks, and environments remains a formidable engineering challenge.

The future of robotics and AI will be defined by further integration of cognitive and embodied intelligence, improved real-world adaptability, and increased autonomy. Sim2Real approaches will continue to evolve, reducing reliance on physical testing, while advancements in neuromorphic computing, on-device AI, and distributed robotic systems will enable real-time, energy-efficient intelligence. Robots will become more collaborative, adaptive, and capable of learning continuously from interactions with humans, the environment, and other agents. Ultimately, the combination of AI and robotics promises not only to enhance efficiency and productivity but to create machines capable of complex reasoning, creativity, and autonomous decision-making in domains previously accessible only to human intelligence.

Conclusion

Robotics combined with AI represents one of the most transformative frontiers of modern technology. Cognitive robotics endows machines with the ability to perceive, reason, and learn from experience, while embodied AI situates intelligence within physical bodies capable of interacting with the environment. Sim2Real advancements bridge the gap between simulation and reality, accelerating skill acquisition while mitigating risk and cost. Together, these developments are shaping a new generation of robots that are not only tools but autonomous agents capable of complex reasoning, collaboration, and adaptive action. As AI continues to evolve and integrate with robotics, the boundaries between software intelligence and physical agency blur, ushering in an era where intelligent machines act, perceive, and think in ways that were once the exclusive domain of humans.

PART III – NEW INDUSTRIES AND APPLICATIONS

CHAPTER 10 – AI IN ENGINEERING AND INFRASTRUCTURE

Introduction

The convergence of artificial intelligence and engineering marks a transformative era in the design, construction, operation, and maintenance of infrastructure. Traditionally, engineering has relied on deterministic models, standardized simulations, and human expertise to conceive and manage structures, systems, and networks. While these methods have enabled remarkable achievements—from skyscrapers and bridges to power grids and transportation networks—they also face increasing challenges. Modern infrastructure projects are more complex than ever, integrating multiple disciplines, massive datasets, environmental constraints, and stringent safety and sustainability requirements. Human decision-making alone is often insufficient to handle the sheer scale, interdependencies, and uncertainty inherent in contemporary engineering projects.

AI introduces a new paradigm by enabling machines to process vast amounts of data, recognize patterns, predict system behavior, and optimize design and operations in ways that were previously impossible. Its role in engineering is no longer confined to incremental automation or design assistance; AI now has the capacity to influence fundamental decisions, accelerate innovation, and improve resilience. From predictive maintenance of bridges to real-time traffic management and automated design optimization, AI is redefining the lifecycle of infrastructure projects. The fusion of computational power, advanced algorithms, and intelligent sensing allows engineers to move beyond static models toward adaptive, data-driven, and self-improving systems.

The integration of AI into engineering also accelerates the shift from reactive to proactive management. Traditionally, engineers responded to failures, delays, and inefficiencies after they occurred. AI enables predictive insights, risk assessment, and scenario analysis that anticipate problems before they manifest. Furthermore, the use of AI in simulation, modeling, and automation supports sustainability goals by optimizing material usage, energy consumption, and lifecycle performance. The adoption of AI in engineering is not simply a technological enhancement; it represents a philosophical shift in how human knowledge, computational intelligence, and physical infrastructure interact.

Structural Engineering

Structural engineering, which forms the backbone of civil and mechanical infrastructure, has historically relied on analytical methods, finite element modeling, and empirical design codes. These approaches, while robust, often struggle with complex, non-linear, or large-scale systems where uncertainty and variability can significantly impact performance. AI offers a new approach by enabling models that learn from real-world data, adapt to changing conditions, and provide predictive insights that complement traditional engineering calculations.

One of the most impactful applications of AI in structural engineering is predictive modeling for structural health monitoring. Sensors embedded in buildings, bridges, dams, and towers continuously generate data on stress, strain, vibration, temperature, and environmental loads. AI algorithms process these streams in real time, identifying subtle patterns that indicate potential failures, material fatigue, or structural degradation. Unlike periodic inspections, AI-enabled monitoring provides continuous oversight, enabling maintenance to be scheduled precisely when needed, reducing costs and preventing catastrophic failures. In earthquake-prone regions, for example, AI can analyze tremor data and structural responses to predict which components are at greatest risk, enhancing safety and resilience.

AI also assists in structural design optimization. Using generative design frameworks powered by neural networks and evolutionary algorithms, engineers can explore millions of design permutations that satisfy multiple criteria, such as material efficiency, load-bearing capacity, and environmental impact. These systems identify non-intuitive solutions that traditional methods might overlook, allowing for lighter, stronger, and more sustainable structures. In addition, AI helps integrate multidisciplinary constraints, considering interactions between structural, electrical, and mechanical systems, which is critical in large infrastructure projects like airports, industrial complexes, or urban developments.

Another significant development is AI-assisted risk assessment. Structural engineers must account for uncertainty in material properties, load conditions, and environmental influences. Machine learning models trained on historical project data, inspection records, and environmental datasets can quantify probabilities of failure under various scenarios. This probabilistic approach complements deterministic design codes, offering a more comprehensive view of safety and reliability. In essence, AI does not replace human expertise; it amplifies it, enabling engineers to make more informed, data-driven decisions across the entire lifecycle of structural systems.

Simulation + AI

Simulation has long been a cornerstone of engineering, allowing professionals to model physical systems, test hypotheses, and predict performance before committing to construction or deployment. Traditional simulations, whether computational fluid dynamics, structural finite element analysis, or thermal modeling, are computationally expensive, time-consuming, and often limited in scale. AI enhances simulation by either accelerating computation, improving accuracy, or extending predictive capabilities to scenarios that are otherwise intractable.

One key advancement is the use of surrogate modeling, where machine learning models approximate complex physical simulations. Neural networks, Gaussian processes, and other AI models can be trained on simulation outputs to create fast-running predictive models. Engineers can then explore a vast range of parameters, design variations, and environmental conditions in minutes rather than days or weeks. This capability enables real-time decision support, rapid optimization, and interactive design evaluation that was impossible with traditional methods alone.

Another significant contribution is hybrid simulation, which combines physics-based modeling with data-driven AI. Purely physics-based simulations often struggle with incomplete data or complex interactions, while purely AI-driven models may fail to honor physical laws. By integrating the two, engineers achieve the best of both worlds: simulations that respect known physics while learning from observed data to refine predictions, capture uncertainties, and handle non-linearities. This approach is particularly valuable in infrastructure exposed to dynamic loads, climate variability, or other complex conditions where traditional models may be insufficient.

AI also enhances stochastic and probabilistic simulations. In areas such as seismic performance, wind loading, flood modeling, or traffic flow analysis, multiple uncertain variables interact in complex ways. Monte Carlo simulations have been traditionally used to explore these uncertainties, but they are computationally intensive. AI models can accelerate sampling, identify critical regions of parameter space, and predict outcomes more efficiently, allowing engineers to assess risk and optimize performance across millions of scenarios. By combining simulation and AI, the engineering profession gains the ability to model infrastructure in unprecedented detail, leading to safer, more efficient, and more adaptive systems.

Digital Twins and Real-Time Automation

Digital twins are virtual replicas of physical infrastructure that integrate real-time sensor data, simulation models, and predictive algorithms. They serve as dynamic mirrors of the physical world, allowing engineers to monitor, analyze, and control systems continuously. AI plays a central role in digital twin technology by enabling real-time processing of sensor data, predictive analytics, anomaly detection, and decision support. In essence, digital twins transform static designs and historical records into living, adaptive systems that evolve alongside their physical counterparts.

Real-time automation in infrastructure relies heavily on these AI-enabled digital twins. In smart cities, for example, digital twins of transportation networks analyze traffic flows, optimize signal timing, and predict congestion before it occurs. In energy systems, digital twins of power grids enable dynamic load balancing, predictive maintenance of transformers, and adaptive responses to renewable generation variability. In industrial facilities, digital twins of plants and machinery allow for continuous monitoring of performance, automatic adjustment of processes, and rapid detection of deviations from optimal operation. By connecting AI to these virtual replicas, engineers can intervene proactively, making decisions that optimize efficiency, safety, and sustainability.

AI-driven digital twins also enhance infrastructure resilience and adaptability. Bridges, tunnels, and high-rise buildings can be monitored continuously for structural stress, vibration, and environmental conditions. The AI system analyzes trends over time and predicts potential failures, allowing for targeted interventions long before damage becomes critical. Similarly, transportation hubs or airports can simulate the impact of unexpected events—such as equipment failures, natural disasters, or sudden surges in demand—and automatically adjust operational strategies. These capabilities transform infrastructure from static, reactive systems into dynamic, self-monitoring entities capable of intelligent adaptation.

The combination of digital twins and AI also supports the concept of continuous learning in infrastructure. Data from sensors, operational logs, maintenance records, and environmental conditions can feed AI algorithms that refine models, optimize decision-making, and improve predictive accuracy over time. This creates a feedback loop where infrastructure learns from its own performance, adapting design, operation, and maintenance strategies iteratively. The result is a future where engineering is not only predictive and analytical but also self-improving, capable of optimizing performance across both daily operations and long-term lifecycle planning.

Conclusion

AI is fundamentally transforming engineering and infrastructure by enhancing prediction, optimization, and automation across the design, construction, and operational phases. In structural engineering, AI enables predictive maintenance, generative design, and probabilistic risk assessment. In simulation, AI accelerates computation, integrates physics with data-driven models, and facilitates analysis of complex, uncertain systems. Through digital twins and real-time automation, AI allows infrastructure to monitor itself, adapt to changing conditions, and continuously improve performance. Collectively, these technologies represent a shift from static, human-driven engineering practices to intelligent, adaptive systems that can perceive, reason, and act autonomously.

The adoption of AI in engineering also introduces broader societal benefits: improved safety, reduced material and energy consumption, enhanced operational efficiency, and greater resilience to natural and man-made disruptions. As AI systems continue to evolve, they will not only assist engineers but also redefine the very nature of infrastructure, transforming roads, bridges, buildings, power networks, and industrial facilities into intelligent, responsive, and self-optimizing systems. The integration of AI in engineering is not simply a technological upgrade—it is the dawn of a new era where infrastructure itself becomes a living, learning system, enabling societies to construct, operate, and maintain resilient environments at unprecedented scale and efficiency.

CHAPTER 11 – AI IN ENERGY AND TRANSPORTATION

Introduction

Energy and transportation are two of the most critical pillars of modern society, underpinning economic development, mobility, and quality of life. Yet both sectors face increasingly complex challenges. Energy systems must integrate intermittent renewable sources, manage aging infrastructure, optimize consumption, and ensure reliability and sustainability. Transportation networks, from highways to railways to urban transit, grapple with congestion, safety, environmental impact, and real-time coordination of vehicles. Artificial intelligence is emerging as a transformative tool for these domains, enabling predictive management, optimization, and autonomy at scales that were previously impossible.

AI in energy and transportation is not merely about automation; it is about intelligence embedded in systems that can learn from data, predict outcomes, and adapt to changing conditions. Sensors, IoT devices, smart grids, connected vehicles, and mobile applications generate continuous streams of information. AI algorithms process this data in real time, providing insights, forecasts, and decision-making capabilities that allow operators to optimize operations, prevent failures, and reduce costs. The fusion of AI with energy and transportation infrastructure promises not only efficiency but resilience, sustainability, and enhanced safety.

AI in Energy Management

Modern energy systems are increasingly complex, integrating traditional fossil fuel sources with solar, wind, hydro, and emerging storage technologies. AI is revolutionizing energy management by enabling predictive forecasting, optimization of generation and consumption, and real-time decision-making.

Predictive algorithms analyze historical usage, weather patterns, and renewable generation forecasts to anticipate demand fluctuations, allowing operators to adjust production proactively. This reduces reliance on reserve capacity, minimizes waste, and optimizes costs.

AI also enhances grid stability. Power grids are vulnerable to disturbances from fluctuating loads, renewable intermittency, and unexpected failures. Machine learning models can detect anomalies in sensor data from transformers, substations, and transmission lines, predicting faults before they escalate. This predictive capability enables preventive maintenance and reduces unplanned outages. Furthermore, AI-driven optimization can balance energy distribution dynamically, rerouting power, managing energy storage systems, and coordinating distributed generation in real time. By integrating AI into energy management, utilities can achieve higher reliability, lower emissions, and improved efficiency.

The integration of AI with demand-side management is equally transformative. Smart meters, home energy management systems, and industrial IoT sensors allow AI to optimize consumption patterns, reducing peak demand and enhancing energy efficiency. For example, AI algorithms can automatically adjust heating, cooling, and industrial machinery operation based on real-time data, occupancy, and pricing signals. This symbiotic relationship between AI and energy systems creates a responsive, adaptive network capable of balancing efficiency, cost, and sustainability goals.

Smart Grids and Renewable Integration

The transition to renewable energy sources introduces variability that traditional grid management struggles to handle. Solar and wind generation fluctuate with weather and time of day, challenging conventional load balancing and forecasting methods. AI provides the tools to manage this complexity. By analyzing meteorological data, sensor inputs, and historical generation trends, AI models can predict renewable output with high accuracy, allowing grid operators to plan load distribution and storage utilization more effectively.

AI also enables the creation of smart grids, where sensors, controllers, and algorithms work together to optimize energy flow dynamically. In a smart grid, energy can be distributed efficiently across regions, storage units can be deployed intelligently, and consumption patterns can be influenced to match generation availability. Machine learning techniques identify consumption patterns, detect anomalies, and enable automated demand response programs that reduce peak loads. AI-driven smart grids not only support renewable integration but also enhance grid resilience, allowing networks to recover quickly from disturbances or outages.

Microgrids and distributed energy systems further benefit from AI. In localized grids serving communities, industrial campuses, or remote areas, AI optimizes the coordination of solar panels, wind turbines, batteries, and conventional generators. These systems can operate independently of the main grid if necessary, responding autonomously to changes in demand, supply, or fault conditions. AI thus transforms energy infrastructure from static, centrally controlled systems to adaptive, distributed, and intelligent networks capable of supporting modern sustainability goals.

AI in Transportation Planning

Transportation systems, from urban transit to highways and railways, face growing pressure due to population growth, urbanization, and increasing mobility demands. AI provides unprecedented tools for planning and optimizing these networks. By analyzing historical traffic data, real-time sensor inputs, GPS trajectories, and social patterns, AI models can identify congestion hotspots, optimize traffic light timing, and suggest route improvements. Predictive analytics allows operators to anticipate demand surges, plan maintenance schedules, and manage incidents proactively.

Beyond operational efficiency, AI supports strategic transportation planning. Urban planners use AI simulations to evaluate the impact of new infrastructure projects, assess public transit capacity, and optimize multimodal networks. Machine learning models can forecast future transportation needs based on population growth, economic trends, and land-use patterns, enabling smarter investment decisions. By integrating AI into both planning and operations, transportation systems become more responsive, sustainable, and capable of meeting the evolving mobility demands of modern cities.

Autonomous and Connected Vehicles

One of the most visible applications of AI in transportation is autonomous vehicles. Self-driving cars, trucks, buses, and drones rely on AI to perceive their environment, make decisions, and act safely. Computer vision, sensor fusion, deep learning, and reinforcement learning enable vehicles to detect obstacles, recognize traffic signs, predict pedestrian movement, and plan safe trajectories. Unlike traditional systems, autonomous vehicles learn from vast datasets and continuously improve their driving policies through simulation and real-world operation.

Connected vehicle technologies amplify AI's impact by enabling real-time communication between vehicles, infrastructure, and cloud services. AI-driven coordination allows traffic to flow more efficiently, reduces congestion, enhances safety, and enables cooperative behavior among autonomous fleets. Predictive algorithms anticipate traffic patterns, while dynamic routing ensures vehicles avoid delays, minimizing fuel consumption and emissions. In logistics, AI-powered fleets optimize delivery routes, manage load balancing, and adapt to unforeseen obstacles, fundamentally transforming goods transportation.

Simulation and Digital Twins in Mobility

Simulation and digital twin technology play an increasingly important role in energy and transportation systems. For autonomous vehicles, high-fidelity simulation allows testing of complex driving scenarios, edge cases, and safety-critical situations without endangering humans. Digital twins of roads, rail networks, and transit systems create virtual replicas that integrate sensor data, traffic analytics, and operational models. AI continuously updates these twins, enabling operators to monitor infrastructure performance, anticipate failures, and optimize flow in real time.

In energy-intensive transportation, such as electric vehicle fleets or rail systems, digital twins help predict battery consumption, maintenance needs, and system interactions. AI algorithms analyze both real-world operations and simulation data to refine planning, reduce downtime, and improve efficiency. These virtual models not only accelerate deployment and innovation but also support long-term decision-making, allowing operators to optimize performance across the entire lifecycle of infrastructure and vehicles.

Sustainability and Future Outlook

AI in energy and transportation is not only about efficiency and performance; it is central to sustainability. By optimizing energy generation, distribution, and consumption, AI reduces waste and carbon emissions. Autonomous and connected vehicles improve fuel efficiency, minimize congestion, and support the transition to electric mobility. Smart grids, predictive maintenance, and demand-side optimization ensure that resources are used responsibly while maintaining reliability.

The future promises further integration of AI with renewable energy, autonomous fleets, and adaptive transportation networks. AI may orchestrate energy flow across interconnected grids, manage multi-modal urban mobility systems, and enable vehicle-to-grid interactions where cars actively stabilize power networks. Edge AI, real-time analytics, and distributed intelligence will allow these systems to operate efficiently, securely, and autonomously. Energy and transportation will become not just automated but intelligent, learning continuously from data to improve performance, reduce environmental impact, and create resilient, adaptive infrastructure.

Conclusion

Artificial intelligence is transforming energy and transportation by enabling predictive management, real-time optimization, autonomous operation, and adaptive planning. AI empowers smart grids to balance renewable sources, anticipate demand, and improve resilience. In transportation, AI drives autonomous vehicles, optimizes traffic, enhances logistics, and supports digital twins for real-time decision-making. By embedding intelligence into both sectors, we are moving from reactive, manually managed systems toward autonomous, self-optimizing networks that are efficient, safe, and sustainable. The integration of AI in energy and transportation represents a profound evolution, reshaping industries that underpin modern society and laying the foundation for a future where intelligent systems actively manage the flow of power, people, and goods across the globe.

CHAPTER 12 – AI IN HEALTHCARE AND LIFE SCIENCES

Introduction

Healthcare and life sciences have always been data-intensive fields, yet the sheer volume, complexity, and diversity of biomedical information have historically outpaced human capacity to process it effectively. Patient records, imaging studies, genomics, clinical trial data, and real-time monitoring streams create opportunities for deeper insight, but traditional analysis methods often fall short. Artificial intelligence promises to transform these sectors by extracting actionable knowledge, predicting outcomes, optimizing care, and accelerating discovery in ways previously unimaginable.

AI in healthcare is more than a tool for automation; it represents a fundamental shift toward precision, personalization, and proactive decision-making. Algorithms can process terabytes of multimodal data, identify subtle correlations invisible to human eyes, and continuously learn from new inputs. The integration of AI into clinical workflows, research pipelines, and public health systems is redefining how we detect disease, develop therapies, manage populations, and deliver care, moving the industry from reactive intervention to anticipatory, data-driven health management.

Clinical Diagnostics and Imaging

One of the earliest and most impactful applications of AI in healthcare is clinical diagnostics, particularly medical imaging. Radiology, pathology, dermatology, and ophthalmology generate vast amounts of image data daily, and accurate interpretation is critical for patient outcomes. AI algorithms, especially deep convolutional neural networks, excel at recognizing patterns in images, identifying abnormalities, and quantifying structures with precision. In practice, AI can detect tumors, fractures, retinal damage, or cardiac anomalies faster and, in some cases, more accurately than human experts, particularly in high-volume screening settings.

Beyond simple detection, AI enhances diagnostic workflows by integrating multimodal information. For instance, combining imaging data with electronic health records, laboratory results, and genomic information enables more nuanced risk stratification and personalized treatment planning. AI-assisted diagnostics reduce human error, streamline interpretation, and allow clinicians to focus on complex decision-making and patient care. Importantly, these systems serve as decision support rather than replacements, amplifying human expertise while maintaining clinical accountability.

Personalized Medicine and Genomics

The era of personalized medicine relies heavily on understanding individual variability in genetics, proteomics, and metabolomics. AI plays a transformative role in analyzing high-dimensional omics datasets, identifying patterns, and predicting how patients will respond to specific treatments. Machine learning models can stratify patients for targeted therapies, predict adverse drug reactions, and suggest optimal treatment regimens tailored to an individual's genetic profile, lifestyle, and medical history.

AI also accelerates genomics research and drug discovery. Sequencing billions of nucleotides produces vast datasets that are impossible to analyze manually. AI models can identify disease-associated variants, predict functional impacts, and reveal new molecular targets for therapy. In oncology, for example, AI analyzes tumor genomics and transcriptomics to guide precision oncology programs, matching patients with the most effective drugs or clinical trials. By linking genomic insight with phenotypic outcomes, AI bridges the gap between molecular biology and clinical intervention, enabling a more personalized and effective approach to healthcare.

Drug Discovery and Development

Traditional drug discovery is time-consuming, costly, and uncertain, often taking over a decade to bring a new therapy to market. AI is reshaping this process by streamlining target identification, compound screening, and preclinical evaluation. Generative models, reinforcement learning, and deep learning algorithms can predict molecular properties, optimize chemical structures, and simulate drug-target interactions before compounds are synthesized in the laboratory.

AI also enhances clinical trial design. By analyzing historical trials, real-world data, and patient registries, algorithms can identify optimal patient cohorts, predict recruitment challenges, and forecast potential side effects. Adaptive trials leverage AI to monitor data in real time, allowing modifications to dosing, inclusion criteria, or endpoints while maintaining scientific rigor. These capabilities reduce costs, improve efficiency, and increase the probability of success, accelerating the pace at which safe and effective therapies reach patients.

Remote Monitoring and Predictive Healthcare

The proliferation of wearable devices, mobile health applications, and IoT-enabled sensors has created continuous streams of patient data, from heart rate and glucose levels to sleep patterns and physical activity. AI algorithms analyze this information to provide predictive insights, detect early warning signs, and support chronic disease management. For example, AI models can anticipate cardiac events, blood sugar excursions, or respiratory distress, prompting timely interventions that prevent hospitalization or severe complications.

Predictive healthcare extends beyond individuals to populations. AI analyzes epidemiological data, environmental factors, and social determinants of health to forecast disease outbreaks, optimize resource allocation, and guide public health interventions. In pandemic response scenarios, AI can model infection spread, identify high-risk regions, and simulate policy impacts. The combination of continuous monitoring, predictive analytics, and proactive intervention represents a profound shift from reactive medicine to anticipatory healthcare, potentially improving outcomes at both individual and societal levels.

Robotics, Automation, and Surgical AI

Robotics and AI have increasingly converged in the surgical and clinical environment. Robot-assisted surgery, guided by AI, enhances precision, reduces human error, and supports minimally invasive procedures. Machine learning models analyze intraoperative imaging, anatomical variations, and patient-specific data to assist surgeons in real time, providing guidance for optimal incision paths, tissue resection, and suture placement.

Beyond the operating room, AI-driven automation improves laboratory workflows, pharmacy operations, and hospital logistics. Automated systems powered by AI can process samples, manage inventory, and optimize scheduling, increasing efficiency and reducing operational errors. Robotics integrated with AI also supports rehabilitation, elderly care, and physical therapy, offering adaptive assistance tailored to patient needs. Together, these technologies extend AI's impact from prediction and diagnosis to physical intervention and healthcare delivery.

Challenges, Ethics, and Future Directions

Despite its transformative potential, AI in healthcare faces significant challenges. Data privacy, regulatory compliance, bias, and explainability remain critical issues. Healthcare decisions have life-or-death consequences, making transparency and accountability essential. Bias in training data can lead to unequal treatment outcomes, requiring rigorous validation, monitoring, and governance. Integrating AI into existing clinical workflows without disrupting care delivery also requires careful design and clinician training.

Looking forward, the integration of AI in healthcare and life sciences promises increasingly personalized, predictive, and adaptive care. The next wave will see AI systems capable of continuous learning from global datasets, real-time patient monitoring, and autonomous intervention support. Digital twins of patients, combining genomic, physiological, and environmental data, could enable simulations of treatment outcomes before interventions are administered. AI will not replace human clinicians but will augment their capabilities, allowing them to deliver higher-quality, more precise, and proactive care.

Conclusion

Artificial intelligence is redefining healthcare and life sciences by enabling precision medicine, accelerating drug discovery, improving diagnostics, and supporting predictive, data-driven care. From genomics and personalized therapies to remote monitoring, robotics, and autonomous clinical support, AI enhances both the efficiency and efficacy of healthcare systems. By integrating real-time data, predictive modeling, and continuous learning, AI transforms reactive care into proactive, anticipatory systems capable of improving patient outcomes and global health resilience.

CHAPTER 13 – AI IN FINANCE AND BUSINESS

Introduction

Finance and business are among the most data-intensive and decision-driven domains in the modern economy. Every day, organizations generate massive volumes of financial transactions, market signals, operational data, customer interactions, and global economic indicators. Making sense of this information to drive strategy, manage risk, optimize performance, and create value is an increasingly complex challenge. Artificial intelligence has emerged as a transformative force in these sectors, enabling predictive insights, automated decision-making, and strategic foresight at scales and speeds unattainable by humans alone.

AI in finance and business is not merely a tool for automation; it fundamentally reshapes decision-making processes. Algorithms can detect patterns across historical and real-time data, anticipate market trends, assess creditworthiness, optimize pricing, and identify operational inefficiencies. By augmenting human intelligence with machine intelligence, AI helps organizations move from reactive responses to proactive, strategic action. In competitive markets, this capability is not optional—it is becoming essential for survival and growth.

AI in Banking and Financial Services

The financial services industry has long relied on data for decision-making, risk assessment, and regulatory compliance. AI amplifies these capabilities by processing vast, complex datasets with unprecedented speed and accuracy. In banking, AI is applied to fraud detection, credit scoring, customer service, algorithmic trading, and portfolio management. Fraud detection systems use machine learning models to analyze transaction patterns and identify anomalies that suggest unauthorized activity. Unlike traditional rule-based systems, AI can detect subtle and evolving threats, continuously adapting as fraudsters develop new tactics.

Credit scoring and lending decisions have also been transformed. Machine learning models can evaluate creditworthiness by analyzing a wide array of variables, from transaction histories and repayment patterns to social behavior and alternative data sources. This enables more accurate risk assessment, faster approvals, and financial inclusion for previously underserved populations. In investment management, AI algorithms process market data, news, and economic indicators to generate predictive insights, optimize portfolio allocation, and execute trades automatically based on real-time conditions. Across banking and finance, AI enhances efficiency, reduces risk, and supports data-driven decision-making at scale.

Predictive Analytics and Business Intelligence

Business intelligence relies on the ability to extract insights from operational data, customer behavior, and market dynamics. AI enhances predictive analytics by identifying trends, forecasting demand, and anticipating operational or market disruptions. Machine learning models can process data from multiple sources—sales records, inventory systems, supply chains, social media, and global economic indicators—to reveal correlations and opportunities that humans might overlook.

Predictive analytics enables proactive decision-making. For instance, retailers can anticipate product demand across regions, optimize inventory allocation, and reduce waste. Manufacturers can predict machine failures and schedule maintenance before costly downtime occurs. AI-powered insights also drive strategic planning by forecasting market shifts, competitor behavior, and regulatory impacts. Organizations equipped with predictive intelligence gain a competitive advantage by acting on foresight rather than reacting to events as they unfold.

AI-Driven Marketing and Customer Engagement

Customer behavior has become increasingly complex, driven by digital interactions, social networks, and personalized expectations. AI allows businesses to understand, anticipate, and influence customer behavior with unprecedented precision. By analyzing transactional data, browsing patterns, sentiment from social media, and engagement metrics, AI can segment audiences, personalize messaging, and predict purchase intent.

Recommendation engines, such as those used in e-commerce, media, and financial platforms, leverage AI to suggest products, services, or content that align with individual preferences. Chatbots and virtual assistants provide instant, intelligent support to customers, enhancing experience while reducing operational costs. Moreover, AI-powered marketing analytics measure campaign effectiveness, identify emerging trends, and optimize strategies in real time. This integration of AI into customer engagement transforms interactions from generic, static experiences into personalized, adaptive, and predictive relationships.

Operational Optimization and Process Automation

AI also drives efficiency and effectiveness within internal business operations. Robotic process automation (RPA), when combined with AI, allows organizations to automate repetitive, rule-based tasks while simultaneously adapting to changing conditions. Invoice processing, procurement, payroll management, and compliance reporting can all benefit from AI-driven automation. Unlike traditional RPA, AI-enhanced systems can interpret documents, understand context, and make judgment-based decisions, increasing flexibility and reducing errors.

Operational optimization extends beyond administrative tasks. AI can optimize supply chains by predicting demand, managing inventory, routing shipments, and identifying bottlenecks. In manufacturing, AI-powered systems monitor equipment performance, optimize production schedules, and minimize downtime. Across operations, AI provides a layer of intelligence that continuously learns from data, improving efficiency, reducing costs, and supporting decision-making at every level of the organization.

Risk Management and Compliance

Risk is inherent to business, whether in financial transactions, operational processes, or strategic decisions. AI enhances risk management by providing predictive analytics, anomaly detection, and scenario modeling. In finance, AI evaluates credit risk, market volatility, and exposure to systemic shocks, allowing firms to hedge and allocate resources effectively. In insurance, AI predicts claims, assesses fraud potential, and optimizes pricing strategies.

Regulatory compliance is another area where AI has profound impact. Regulatory reporting, anti-money laundering (AML) checks, and fraud investigations often involve vast datasets and complex rules. AI systems can process these efficiently, flagging potential violations and enabling auditors and regulators to focus on high-risk areas. By improving accuracy, speed, and consistency, AI reduces operational and regulatory risk while ensuring compliance in increasingly complex regulatory environments.

Algorithmic Trading and Investment Management

Financial markets generate vast quantities of high-frequency data, and decisions must often be made in milliseconds. AI-driven algorithmic trading uses deep learning, reinforcement learning, and predictive analytics to execute trades, identify arbitrage opportunities, and manage risk dynamically. These systems adapt to changing market conditions, learning from historical and real-time data to improve performance continuously.

In investment management, AI enables portfolio optimization, asset allocation, and scenario planning. By analyzing correlations, risk factors, and macroeconomic indicators, AI models provide investment insights that are more data-driven and adaptive than traditional methods. For hedge funds, wealth management, and institutional investors, AI improves returns, reduces volatility, and enhances responsiveness to rapidly changing market conditions. The integration of AI into trading and investment transforms markets from reactive environments into intelligent, data-driven systems.

AI in Strategic Decision-Making

Beyond operational and financial applications, AI increasingly informs strategic business decisions. Executives can leverage AI to simulate market scenarios, evaluate new product launches, assess mergers and acquisitions, and identify emerging opportunities or threats. Machine learning models can synthesize internal data with global market intelligence, competitor activity, and geopolitical trends, providing actionable insights for long-term planning.

Strategic AI also supports scenario analysis and forecasting under uncertainty. Businesses can model multiple "what-if" scenarios, from supply chain disruptions to regulatory changes, and evaluate the potential impact on revenue, cost, and risk. By combining predictive intelligence with human judgment, AI enables more informed and confident decision-making at the highest levels, aligning operations with strategic goals in complex, dynamic markets.

Future Outlook and Emerging Trends

The future of AI in finance and business will extend beyond automation and analytics into autonomous decision-making and real-time optimization. Organizations will increasingly deploy AI agents capable of continuously monitoring markets, optimizing operations, and executing decisions with minimal human intervention. Edge AI and real-time analytics will allow decisions to be made at the point of action, from retail floors to trading desks to industrial operations.

Explainable AI will become essential as regulatory bodies demand transparency in decision-making, especially in financial and customer-facing applications. Integration with blockchain, IoT, and distributed ledger systems will further enhance trust, traceability, and operational efficiency. AI will also facilitate adaptive enterprises—organizations that learn continuously from data, adapt strategies dynamically, and respond to market changes faster than competitors. The next decade promises not just smarter analytics but autonomous, intelligent organizations that operate with unprecedented agility and insight.

Conclusion

AI is fundamentally transforming finance and business, enhancing decision-making, optimizing operations, managing risk, and enabling strategic foresight. From banking and investment management to marketing, supply chains, and compliance, AI allows organizations to process vast data streams, detect patterns, and act proactively. Algorithmic trading, predictive analytics, operational automation, and strategic scenario modeling demonstrate the breadth of AI applications. As AI continues to evolve, it will drive the emergence of intelligent, adaptive enterprises capable of continuous learning, autonomous decision-making, and real-time responsiveness. The integration of AI into finance and business is not merely a technological shift—it is a structural transformation that reshapes how organizations create value, manage risk, and compete in a dynamic global economy.

CHAPTER 14 – AI IN EDUCATION AND KNOWLEDGE WORK

Introduction

Education and knowledge work are undergoing profound transformation as artificial intelligence becomes deeply integrated into learning, research, and professional productivity. Traditional models of education often struggle to address the diversity of learners, the rapid expansion of knowledge, and the need for personalized guidance. Similarly, knowledge workers in business, science, engineering, and creative industries face the challenge of managing enormous volumes of data, extracting insights, and producing outputs with both speed and accuracy. AI offers tools to augment human cognition, optimize learning and research, and redefine how knowledge is created, shared, and applied.

In both education and knowledge work, AI is shifting the paradigm from passive consumption to active, adaptive engagement. Intelligent systems can analyze learning patterns, identify gaps, suggest personalized resources, and provide instant feedback. In professional contexts, AI can automate routine tasks, assist in complex problem solving, and generate insights from unstructured data. By embedding intelligence into workflows and educational platforms, AI enables humans to focus on creativity, critical thinking, and strategic judgment, enhancing productivity and learning outcomes simultaneously.

Personalized Learning and Adaptive Education

One of the most visible impacts of AI in education is personalized learning. Every student has unique strengths, weaknesses, learning styles, and paces. Traditional classrooms often adopt a one-size-fits-all approach, which can leave some learners behind while under-challenging others. AI-powered adaptive learning systems address this challenge by continuously analyzing student interactions, performance data, and engagement metrics to tailor content and exercises to individual needs.

These systems can provide instant feedback, highlight misconceptions, and suggest targeted resources, ensuring that learning is both effective and efficient. For example, AI tutors can adjust the difficulty of problems in real time, recommend supplementary materials, or offer alternative explanations when students struggle. This personalized approach not only enhances understanding but also fosters motivation, engagement, and long-term retention, transforming education into a learner-centric experience that evolves dynamically with each student.

Intelligent Tutoring and Virtual Assistants

Beyond adaptive learning platforms, AI has enabled the emergence of intelligent tutoring systems and virtual teaching assistants. These AI systems can interact naturally with learners, answer questions, clarify concepts, and provide guidance on assignments. Unlike static instructional content, AI tutors can recognize patterns in student behavior, identify areas of confusion, and adapt explanations to the learner's level of understanding.

In higher education and professional training, AI-powered virtual assistants support instructors by automating grading, monitoring student progress, and providing insights into classroom dynamics. This allows educators to focus on mentorship, discussion, and higher-order instruction. For corporate knowledge work, virtual AI assistants can help employees navigate internal knowledge bases, summarize reports, and answer procedural questions, acting as on-demand advisors that enhance efficiency and learning simultaneously.

AI in Research and Knowledge Discovery

Knowledge work increasingly relies on the ability to process vast volumes of information, identify connections, and generate insights. AI transforms research workflows by analyzing scientific literature, patents, and datasets at scales far beyond human capacity. Natural language processing models can summarize articles, extract key concepts, and map relationships between findings, enabling researchers to navigate the ever-expanding knowledge landscape effectively.

AI also supports hypothesis generation and experimental design. By identifying gaps in existing research and suggesting novel approaches, AI systems can accelerate discovery in science, engineering, and medicine. For example, AI-driven literature analysis has been used to identify potential drug candidates, optimize experimental protocols, and suggest new avenues for exploration. In knowledge-intensive industries, AI acts as an intellectual partner, amplifying human reasoning and creativity while reducing the time and effort required to extract actionable insights.

Automation of Routine Knowledge Work

Knowledge workers spend a significant portion of their time on repetitive, low-value tasks such as data entry, document review, and information synthesis. AI automates these processes, freeing professionals to focus on strategic, creative, and analytical activities. Robotic process automation (RPA) combined with AI can extract data from unstructured sources, classify documents, summarize content, and integrate information across systems, streamlining workflows and improving accuracy.

In law, AI can review contracts and highlight risk clauses; in finance, AI can reconcile accounts and detect anomalies; in journalism, AI can summarize reports and draft preliminary articles. By handling routine work efficiently, AI reduces human error, accelerates productivity, and allows professionals to dedicate attention to higher-order decision-making and innovation.

Collaborative AI and Knowledge Ecosystems

The next wave of AI in knowledge work emphasizes collaboration between humans and intelligent systems. AI can serve as a co-creator, brainstorming ideas, generating drafts, modeling scenarios, and evaluating alternatives. Collaborative AI tools allow teams to interact with large datasets, simulate business strategies, or explore research hypotheses together, enhancing both creativity and rigor.

In education, AI facilitates peer learning and collaborative problem-solving by recommending study partners, forming groups based on complementary skills, or suggesting discussion topics. In professional environments, AI supports cross-functional teams by connecting experts, integrating data across silos, and providing context-specific insights. This collaborative intelligence blurs the line between human and machine contribution, enabling hybrid teams that leverage the strengths of both.

Ethical, Privacy, and Bias Considerations

While AI offers transformative potential in education and knowledge work, it raises critical ethical, privacy, and equity concerns. Adaptive learning systems rely on sensitive personal data, and improper handling can compromise student privacy. AI models can also reflect or amplify biases present in training data, potentially disadvantaging certain learners or groups. In professional settings, reliance on AI for decision-making may obscure accountability, reduce transparency, or introduce systemic biases if not carefully monitored.

Addressing these challenges requires robust governance, transparency, and ongoing validation. Explainable AI, privacy-preserving algorithms, and human oversight are essential to ensure that AI-enhanced education and knowledge work remain equitable, ethical, and aligned with societal values.

Future Directions: Lifelong Learning and Cognitive Augmentation

The integration of AI into education and knowledge work is paving the way for lifelong learning and continuous cognitive augmentation. AI systems will support individuals in acquiring new skills, keeping up with evolving knowledge, and navigating complex professional environments. Personalized learning pathways, AI-curated content, and adaptive skill assessments will allow people to learn efficiently across their careers.

In knowledge work, AI will evolve from a supportive tool to a proactive partner, capable of anticipating information needs, generating insights autonomously, and even guiding strategic decisions. The convergence of AI with augmented reality, virtual collaboration platforms, and cognitive computing will create immersive environments where learning and knowledge creation are seamless, interactive, and adaptive. Professionals and students alike will operate in AI-enhanced ecosystems that amplify human intelligence and creativity continuously.

Conclusion

Artificial intelligence is fundamentally transforming education and knowledge work by personalizing learning, augmenting research, automating routine tasks, and enabling collaborative intelligence. AI-powered adaptive platforms, virtual tutors, and intelligent assistants enhance both learning outcomes and professional productivity, while predictive and analytic capabilities enable more informed decision-making. By embedding AI into workflows, curricula, and knowledge ecosystems, humans gain the ability to focus on creativity, critical thinking, and strategic reasoning, while AI handles data-intensive, repetitive, or complex computational tasks.

As AI continues to advance, it promises a future where education is fully learner-centric, professional work is seamlessly augmented, and knowledge creation becomes faster, more precise, and more innovative. The partnership between humans and AI will not replace expertise but will amplify it, transforming learning, work, and the creation of value across industries and disciplines.

CHAPTER 15 – AI INTEGRATION WITH THE CONSTRUCTION INDUSTRY

Introduction

The construction industry is traditionally labor-intensive, complex, and fragmented. It involves coordination between architects, engineers, contractors, suppliers, and regulatory authorities while managing massive projects that span months or years. Construction projects are prone to delays, cost overruns, safety hazards, and inefficiencies due to the complexity of operations, variability in human performance, and unpredictable environmental factors. Artificial intelligence offers transformative potential in addressing these challenges, creating a future where construction projects are safer, faster, and more efficient.

AI integration in construction is more than automation—it represents the convergence of intelligent planning, predictive analysis, and real-time operational insight. From design to completion, AI can optimize workflows, enhance decision-making, monitor safety, and improve resource allocation. By embedding intelligence into every stage of construction, the industry can achieve higher precision, reduce waste, and enable predictive maintenance and quality assurance, creating a new paradigm of "smart construction."

AI in Design and Planning

The design phase is critical in construction, influencing costs, safety, and feasibility. Traditionally, architects and engineers relied on manual calculations, experience, and standard software tools to generate plans. AI enhances this process by analyzing historical project data, simulating multiple design scenarios, and optimizing structural, mechanical, and energy systems. Machine learning algorithms can evaluate thousands of design variations in minutes, identifying the most efficient, cost-effective, and sustainable solutions.

Generative design tools powered by AI allow architects and engineers to input project constraints—such as site dimensions, material availability, and environmental requirements—and receive optimized designs that satisfy structural, aesthetic, and functional criteria. This accelerates planning cycles and reduces human error. AI also improves collaboration by integrating design feedback from multiple stakeholders, ensuring that architectural, structural, and MEP (mechanical, electrical, and plumbing) systems are harmonized from the outset.

Construction Site Monitoring and Management

Construction sites are dynamic environments where hundreds of tasks occur simultaneously. AI-enabled site monitoring uses computer vision, IoT sensors, and drones to track progress, detect deviations from schedules, and ensure quality compliance. Cameras combined with AI can identify safety hazards such as workers not wearing protective equipment, unauthorized equipment movement, or unstable scaffolding.

By continuously analyzing real-time data, AI provides actionable insights for site managers. Predictive models can estimate completion times for tasks, forecast material shortages, and detect potential bottlenecks. AI-driven dashboards allow supervisors to make informed decisions, allocate resources efficiently, and minimize downtime. This level of oversight transforms construction sites into intelligent ecosystems, where safety, efficiency, and quality are continuously monitored and optimized.

Predictive Maintenance and Equipment Optimization

Construction machinery and equipment are expensive and subject to wear, downtime, and unexpected failures. Traditional maintenance schedules are often reactive or based on fixed intervals, which can lead to costly disruptions. AI enables predictive maintenance by analyzing sensor data from machinery, detecting patterns of wear and tear, and forecasting failures before they occur.

For example, AI systems can monitor engine vibrations, hydraulic performance, and operational temperature, predicting the optimal time for maintenance. This proactive approach reduces equipment downtime, extends asset lifespan, and lowers operational costs. AI can also optimize fleet utilization, assigning the right machines to tasks based on availability, performance, and energy efficiency. Equipment-intensive projects, such as large infrastructure works, benefit significantly from AI-driven maintenance and operational strategies.

Supply Chain and Material Management

Construction projects rely heavily on timely delivery of materials. Delays in the supply chain can halt progress, leading to cost overruns and contractual disputes. AI optimizes supply chain operations by analyzing demand, tracking inventory, and predicting material shortages or surpluses. Machine learning models can forecast material consumption rates based on project plans, site conditions, and past usage patterns.

AI also facilitates procurement by identifying optimal suppliers, predicting delivery times, and recommending cost-effective purchasing strategies. Combined with IoT-enabled tracking of materials, AI ensures that inventory is available when and where it is needed, reducing waste and storage costs. Efficient material management powered by AI is particularly valuable for large-scale or multi-site construction projects where coordination is critical.

Safety and Risk Management

Safety is a paramount concern in construction, with accidents leading to human, financial, and reputational costs. AI enhances safety through real-time monitoring, predictive risk assessment, and proactive hazard prevention. Computer vision systems can detect unsafe behaviors, such as workers in restricted zones or improper use of machinery, and trigger instant alerts.

Predictive analytics models can assess historical accident data, environmental conditions, and human factors to forecast areas of high risk. AI can simulate construction scenarios, identifying potential structural failures, collision hazards, or workflow conflicts before they occur. By integrating AI into safety management systems, organizations move from reactive incident response to proactive prevention, creating safer workplaces and ensuring regulatory compliance.

Digital Twins and Real-Time Simulation

Digital twins—virtual replicas of physical construction sites—represent one of the most powerful applications of AI in construction. By combining AI, IoT sensors, and 3D modeling, digital twins allow managers to monitor site conditions, simulate project workflows, and test design modifications in a virtual environment before implementing them on-site.

AI-driven digital twins can predict the impact of changes in schedules, materials, or labor allocation, providing real-time decision support. They also facilitate collaboration among architects, engineers, contractors, and clients by offering a shared, accurate, and dynamic representation of the project. The integration of AI with digital twins enhances precision, reduces costly errors, and accelerates project timelines, transforming construction into a continuous feedback-driven process.

AI in Construction Robotics

Robotics has gradually entered construction, performing tasks such as bricklaying, concrete pouring, welding, and material transport. AI extends the capabilities of these robots, enabling them to operate autonomously in complex and unpredictable environments. Cognitive robots equipped with AI can navigate dynamic sites, avoid obstacles, and adjust actions based on real-time conditions.

AI-powered robotics enhances productivity and reduces labor-intensive risks. For example, autonomous drones perform aerial inspections of structures, mapping progress, identifying defects, and monitoring environmental conditions. Robotic systems can also collaborate with human workers, handling repetitive or dangerous tasks while humans focus on complex decision-making. This synergy between AI and robotics elevates construction efficiency, safety, and precision.

AI for Sustainability and Energy Efficiency

Modern construction projects face increasing pressure to meet sustainability targets and minimize environmental impact. AI contributes by optimizing material usage, energy consumption, and waste management. Predictive models can estimate energy requirements for construction processes, identify opportunities for renewable energy integration, and suggest materials with lower carbon footprints.

AI also supports lifecycle sustainability planning. By analyzing historical project data and simulating long-term building performance, AI helps architects and engineers design structures that are energy-efficient, resilient, and cost-effective. AI-driven sustainability initiatives not only reduce environmental impact but also improve compliance with green building certifications, offering long-term operational and financial benefits.

Future Directions: Fully Integrated AI Construction Ecosystems

The ultimate vision for AI in construction is a fully integrated ecosystem where planning, execution, monitoring, and maintenance are seamlessly interconnected. In this future, AI systems continuously learn from each project, improving predictive models, refining workflows, and enhancing safety protocols. Autonomous machinery, drones, and robotic systems operate in coordination with human teams, while digital twins provide real-time situational awareness and decision support.

AI will enable end-to-end optimization, from design generation and material sourcing to construction sequencing and post-occupancy monitoring. Projects will be delivered faster, safer, and more sustainably, with reduced costs and enhanced quality. As AI continues to evolve, construction will shift from fragmented, reactive processes to intelligent, predictive, and adaptive systems, redefining what is possible in the built environment.

Conclusion

Artificial intelligence is reshaping the construction industry by introducing intelligence, automation, and predictive capabilities across every stage of a project. From design optimization and predictive maintenance to robotics, digital twins, and sustainability, AI enhances efficiency, safety, and decision-making while reducing costs and errors. The integration of AI into construction represents not just technological advancement but a fundamental transformation of industry practices. As AI adoption deepens, the construction industry will evolve into a smart, adaptive, and highly productive ecosystem where human expertise is amplified by machine intelligence, enabling projects that are safer, faster, more precise, and environmentally responsible.

APPENDICES

GLOSSARY OF AI TERMS

Artificial Intelligence (AI): The simulation of human intelligence processes by machines, including learning, reasoning, and self-correction.

Neural Network: A computing system inspired by the structure of the human brain, used to recognize patterns and make decisions.

Deep Learning: A subset of machine learning using multi-layered neural networks for complex tasks such as image recognition or language understanding.

Foundation Model: Large AI models trained on diverse datasets to perform multiple tasks with minimal task-specific tuning.

Generative AI: AI systems that can create content—text, images, audio, or video—based on patterns learned from data.

Reinforcement Learning: A type of machine learning where an agent learns to make decisions by receiving rewards or penalties from interactions with the environment.

Digital Twin: A virtual representation of a physical system or environment, used for simulation, monitoring, and predictive modeling.

Edge AI: AI computation performed on local devices rather than centralized servers, enabling low-latency decision-making.

Neuro-Symbolic AI: A hybrid approach combining neural networks' learning power with symbolic AI's logical reasoning capabilities.

Agentic AI: AI systems that can act, plan, and learn autonomously within defined environments.

TIMELINE OF AI DEVELOPMENT

- **1943:** Warren McCulloch and Walter Pitts propose the first computational model of a neural network.
- **1956:** Dartmouth Conference coins the term "Artificial Intelligence," formally establishing the field.
- **1960s–1970s:** Early symbolic AI research, including Logic Theorist and ELIZA chatbot experiments.
- **1980s:** Expert systems like MYCIN demonstrate AI's potential in specialized domains.
- **1986:** Introduction of backpropagation for training neural networks.
- **1997:** IBM Deep Blue defeats chess champion Garry Kasparov.
- **2006:** Deep learning revival, enabling breakthroughs in speech and image recognition.
- **2012:** AlexNet wins the ImageNet competition, demonstrating the power of convolutional neural networks.
- **2016:** AlphaGo defeats world champion Go player Lee Sedol.
- **2018–2020:** Emergence of foundation models (e.g., GPT, BERT) enabling transfer learning and multimodal AI.
- **2023–2025:** Rapid adoption of generative AI across industries, AI-driven robotics, autonomous systems, and edge intelligence.

PROFILES OF MAJOR AI RESEARCHERS

- **John McCarthy:** Coined the term "Artificial Intelligence" and advanced early AI logic-based systems.
- **Marvin Minsky:** Co-founder of MIT AI Lab, known for work on knowledge representation and robotics.
- **Geoffrey Hinton:** Pioneer of deep learning and backpropagation; significantly advanced neural networks.
- **Yoshua Bengio:** Key contributor to deep learning architectures and AI theory.
- **Yann LeCun:** Developer of convolutional neural networks and leader in machine vision research.
- **Fei-Fei Li:** Advanced large-scale image recognition, including ImageNet, bridging AI with human perception.
- **Demis Hassabis:** Founder of DeepMind, leader in reinforcement learning and agentic AI systems.

LEARNING RESOURCES AND REFERENCES

Books:

"Artificial Intelligence: A Modern Approach" by Stuart Russell and Peter Norvig

"Deep Learning" by Ian Goodfellow, Yoshua Bengio, and Aaron Courville

"Human Compatible" by Stuart Russell (AI safety and alignment)

Online Courses:

Coursera: "AI For Everyone" by Andrew Ng

edX: "Artificial Intelligence" by Columbia University

DeepLearning.AI specialization courses

Journals and Conferences:

Journal of Artificial Intelligence Research (JAIR)

Neural Information Processing Systems (NeurIPS)

International Conference on Learning Representations (ICLR)

Communities and Resources:

OpenAI Research Blog

AI Stack Exchange

Kaggle competitions for hands-on machine learning practice

Construction-Specific AI Resources:

Journal of Construction Engineering and Management

Automation in Construction (Elsevier)

AI in Building Information Modeling (BIM) white papers

www.ingramcontent.com/pod-product-compliance
Lightning Source LLC
LaVergne TN
LVHW060042210926
848481LV00013B/3931
9798218870607